The GARDEN GOURMET'S

VEGETABLE COOKERY

by
Chef Antonio P. Cabianca

Front Cover Photograph
Asparagus Pecan Salad, page 54

The Garden Gourmet's Vegetable Cookery
by
Chef Antonio P. Cabianca

First Printing — January 1990

Copyright " 1990 by Antonio P. Cabianca

Garden Gourmet Enterprises
P. O. Box 78035
Pharmasave
Port Coquitlam, B.C.
V3B 7H5

Canadian Cataloguing in Publication Data
Cabianca, Antonio P., 1959-

  The garden gourmet's vegetable cookery

  ISBN 0-919845-93-2

1. Cookery (Vegetables). 2. Cookery (Fruit).
I. Title.
TX801.C3 1991 641.6'5 C91-097005-X

Cover Design by
Amanda Maslany Design
Regina, Saskatchewan

Photography by
Patricia Holdsworth Photography
Regina, Saskatchewan

Glass soup plate by Cheryl Spicer
Courtesy of Collections Fine Art Gallery, Regina, Saskatchewan

Wine selection by
Paul Warwick, wine educator/celebrity chef

Designed, Printed and Produced in Canada by:
Centax books, a Division of M•C•Graphics Inc.
Publishing Director, Photo Designer and Food Stylist: Margo Embury
1048 Fleury Street, Regina, Saskatchewan, Canada S4N 4W8
(306) 359-3737 / 359-7580   FAX (306) 525-3955

TABLE OF CONTENTS

H E R B S   &   S P I C E S

For all of you who are always looking for that perfect spice to accent that special vegetable, I have put together some guidelines that may help. I have found that my imagination, plus my professional background and knowledge, worked best for me. Remember, these are not all the vegetables and spices available but they will spark some creative ideas.

Vegetables	Herbs & Spices
Artichokes	bay leaf, savory, tarragon
Asparagus	chervil, chives, dillweed, lemon balm
Avocado	dillweed, marjoram, tarragon, anise seed
Cabbage	caraway, dill seed, marjoram, mint, oregano, parsley, sage, savory, thyme
Carrots	chervil, parsley, mint
Cauliflower	chives, dillweed, fennel, rosemary
Green beans	dillweed, marjoram, mint, oregano, sage, rosemary, savory, tarragon,
Mushrooms	basil, dillweed, lemon balm, marjoram, parsley, rosemary, savory, tarragon, thyme,
Onions	basil, dill, oregano, sage, tarragon, thyme,
Peas	basil, chervil, marjoram, mint, parsley, rosemary, sage, savory
Potatoes	basil, bay leaf, chives, dill, lovage, marjoram, mint, oregano, parsley, rosemary, thyme
Spinach	chervil, marjoram, mint, borage, tarragon, sorrel
Tomato	basil, bay leaf, chervil, chives (all types), dillweed, garlic, mint, marjoram, oregano, parsley, sage, savory, tarragon
Zucchini	basil, garlic, dill, marjoram rosemary, tarragon

Bon Appétit

APPETIZERS

MARINATED ARTICHOKES

serves 4

8	artichoke hearts, cut in half	8
2	eggs, hard-boiled, peeled and sliced	2
2 tbsp.	chopped green onion	30 mL
3-4	okra, 4" (10 cm), washed and sliced	3-4

Depending on the time of year, use bottled, fresh or canned artichoke hearts. If using bottled artichoke hearts, use those that are not seasoned, just packed in oil or water. Combine all ingredients and marinate with the following Herb Garlic Marinade. Chill in refrigerator overnight.

herb garlic marinade

¼ cup	olive oil	50 mL
¼ cup	vinegar or red wine vinegar	50 mL
¼ tsp.	sugar	1 mL
1 tsp.	freshly chopped garlic	5 mL
⅓ tsp.	marjoram	1.5 mL
4 tbsp.	pine nuts	60 mL

Combine all ingredients.

MARINATED MUSHROOMS
with italian marinade

serves 6

½ lb.	white mushrooms	250 g
2	celery stalks, finely minced	2
½	red pepper, finely minced	½
½	green pepper, finely minced	½
¼ cup	sliced black olives	50 mL

Combine mushrooms, celery, red and green peppers, olives and the following Italian Marinade; let sit a minimum of 4-6 hours in the refrigerator.

MARINATED MUSHROOMS
(continued)

italian marinade

1 cup	oil	250 mL
½ cup	vinegar	125 mL
2 tbsp.	minced garlic	30 mL
1 tbsp.	freshly minced oregano	15 mL
½ tbsp.	freshly minced sweet basil	7.5 mL
¼ cup	whole cream (optional)	50 mL

Combine all ingredients, using whole cream only when you want a creamy marinade.

CREAMED CELERY STICKS

makes 14-16

4-5	large stalks of celery	4-5
¼ cup	cream cheese	50 mL
¼ cup	sour cream	50 mL
2 tbsp.	Dijon mustard	30 mL
1 tbsp.	chopped chives	15 mL

Clean celery; cut into halves or thirds. Beat cream cheese until smooth and combine with sour cream, mustard and chives. Fill celery with sour cream mixture; refrigerate until firm.

RAW VEGETABLE PLATTER

serves 2-4

4	broccoli sprigs	4
4	cauliflower sprigs	4
1	celery stalk, cut into thirds, sliced lengthwise	1
½	yellow pepper, cut into thirds	½
½	red pepper, cut into thirds	½
½	green pepper, cut into thirds	½
4	mushrooms	4
4	whole white oyster mushrooms	4
4	carrot sticks	4
4	radishes	4
1	Belgium endive, firm, quartered	4
4	cherry tomatoes	4
4	½" (1.2 cm) slices of cucumbers	4

Arrange vegetables to make an eye-appealing arrangement. Serve with a Cucumber Dill Dip, page 28, and/or a Spicy Cheese Dip, page 28.

AVOCADO MOUSSE

with blackberry hollandaise sauce

serves 6

2 tbsp.	gelatin (2 packets)	30 mL
1 cup	water	250 mL
2	avocados	2
2 tbsp.	lemon juice	30 mL
½ tsp.	salt	2 mL
1 tbsp.	whipping cream	15 mL

Soften gelatin in ½ cup (125 mL) water; heat gelatin to dissolve, adding ½ cup (125 mL) of boiling water. Halve the avocados; remove pit; remove meat from avocado skin and put in food processor with remaining ingredients, including gelatin and water. Blend thoroughly and pour into individual molds. Refrigerate overnight or until set. Remove from molds and top with Blackberry Hollandaise Sauce, page 76.

MUSHROOMS ANTONIO

serves 6-8

½ cup	cream cheese	125 mL
3 tbsp.	crab meat	45 mL
2 tbsp.	shrimp meat	30 mL
1 tbsp.	chopped chives or green onions	15 mL
½ tsp.	lemon juice	2 mL
1 tbsp.	freshly chopped dill	15 mL
	salt and pepper to taste	
½ lb.	white mushrooms, stems removed	125 g

Combine cheese, crab, shrimp, chives, lemon and spices in a food processor and blend until mixed. Fill mushroom caps with seafood mixture; broil until brown. Serve hot with Béarnaise Sauce.

BROILED CELERY BUNDLES

makes 16-18

5	large stalks of celery	5
6	bacon slices	6
¾ cup	butter	175 mL
2	large garlic cloves, minced	2
1 tbsp.	chopped sweet basil	15 mL

Clean celery, cut into thirds, then into fine strips. Take 8 strips and wrap ½ slice bacon around the center of the bundle. Place bundles, seam side down on cookie sheet; top with garlic butter and basil; broil until browned lightly.

variation

You may substitute ½ celery with ½ carrot strips.

B R O I L E D   J A L A P E Ñ O S

serves 4

8	jalapeño peppers, sliced lengthwise, seeded	8
¼ cup	drained crushed pineapple	50 mL
1 tsp.	allspice	5 mL
1 cup	cream cheese	250 mL

Prepare peppers. Combine pineapple, allspice and cream cheese until smooth. Arrange peppers on baking sheet; fill with cream cheese mixture; bake at 450°F (230°C) for 6-12 minutes. Serve with Salsa, page 29, and sour cream.

C A R R O T   &   B E A N   B U N D L E S

serves 6-8

3 tbsp.	butter	45 mL
1	onion, finely diced	1
2½ cups	grated carrots	625 mL
1 cup	French-style cut beans, drained	250 mL
1 cup	ricotta cheese	250 mL
⅓ cup	grated Parmesan cheese	75 mL
2	eggs, beaten	2
¼ cup	fine bread crumbs	50 mL
16 oz.	pkg. phyllo pastry	454 g
	melted butter	

Melt butter; sauté onion. Mix in carrot, beans, cheeses, eggs and bread crumbs. Unroll phyllo pastry, remove 1 sheet and cut in half lengthwise. Cover remaining sheets with a barely dampened tea towel, to keep them supple. Brush half of phyllo strip, lengthwise, with melted butter; fold phyllo lengthwise and brush again with butter. Spoon 1 tbsp. (15 mL) of vegetable mixture across the bottom edge of phyllo. Fold phyllo edges in lengthwise and roll up bundle. Brush with butter as needed and brush finished roll with butter. Place rolls on ungreased baking sheet and bake at 350°F (180°C) until golden brown.

V E G E T A B L E   T A R T L E T S

serves 12

¼ cup	shredded carrot	50 mL
¼ cup	finely chopped chives	50 mL
¼ cup	minced green pepper	50 mL
2	eggs	2
8 oz.	cream cheese	250 g
	salt and pepper to taste	
dash	Worcestershire sauce	
24	tartlet shells	24
	paprika	

Mix all ingredients, except tartlets and paprika, together with a wooden spoon. Fill tartlets. Bake in a 350°F (180°C) oven for 12 to 15 minutes. Sprinkle paprika on top. Serve at once.

D E E P - F R I E D   A R T I C H O K E S

serves 4

batter for deep-frying

1	egg, large	1
1 cup	water, cold	250 mL
1¼ cups	flour	325 mL
	oil for deep-frying	
1 cup	canned or bottled artichoke hearts	250 mL
½ tsp.	oregano	2 mL
½ tsp.	sweet basil	2 mL

Combine egg, water and flour; blend until smooth. Refrigerate overnight. Heat oil to 365°F (185°C). Toss artichokes lightly with herbs. Dip in batter; deep-fry until golden brown. Serve with Green Mayonnaise, page 31.

P R O F I T E R O L E S

serves 6

⅓ cup	flour	75 mL
¼ cup	Parmesan cheese	50 mL
⅛ cup	grated Cheddar cheese	25 mL
⅓ cup	butter	75 mL
2	eggs	2
⅛ cup	grated carrot	25 mL
	oil for frying	

Combine flour and cheeses. Melt butter and add to flour and cheese mixture as quickly as possible, until it stops sticking to the sides. With a wooden spoon, beat in eggs, 1 at a time, until combined; mix in carrots. Heat oil to 365°F (185°C). Drop dough from tablespoon into deep fryer. Fry until golden; drain well on paper towels. Serve immediately.

P O T A T O   C A K E S

serves 6

4 cups	cooked, mashed potatoes	1 kg
1 cup	flour	250 mL
3	eggs	3
¼ cup	vegetable oil	50 mL
½ cup	finely chopped onion	125 mL
¼ cup	finely chopped green onion	50 mL
1 tbsp.	chopped parsley	15 mL
	salt and pepper to taste	
	oil for frying	

Combine all ingredients except oil for frying. DO NOT OVER MIX. Refrigerate for at least 1 hour. Heat 1-2 tbsp. (15-30 mL) of oil in skillet. Drop potato mixture by spoonfuls into skillet. Fry for 6-8 minutes a side, until golden brown. Serve with Corn Relish, page 36, and sour cream.

BEVERAGES

CUCUMBER COCKTAIL

serves 2

4	cucumbers, peeled, chopped	4
1	small onion, chopped	1
2 cups	tomato juice	500 mL
½ tsp.	crushed or ground cumin seed	2 mL
	Worcestershire sauce	
	salt and pepper to taste	
	cucumber sticks for garnish	

Purée cucumber and onion together in food processor. Add to tomato juice; add cumin seed, Worcestershire sauce, salt and pepper to taste. Serve in tall glasses with cracked ice. Garnish with a cucumber stick.

CUCUMBER BUTTERMILK

serves 6

1¼ cups	tomato juice	300 mL
2 cups	buttermilk	500 mL
½ tsp.	curry powder	2 mL
3 dashes	Worcestershire sauce	3 dashes
2	large cucumbers, peeled, finely diced	2

Blend the first 4 ingredients until smooth. Stir in cucumber and pour into cocktail glasses.

SPICY CARROT JUICE

serves 1

2	medium carrots, puréed	2
½ cup	water	125 mL
dash	Worcestershire sauce	dash
	salt and pepper to taste	

Combine carrots and water; add remaining ingredients to taste. Pour into a cracked-ice-filled glass.

CARROT DIVINE

serves 1

2	medium carrots, puréed	2
½ cup	tomato juice	125 mL
dash	Worcestershire sauce	dash
dash	Tabasco	dash
	salt and pepper to taste	

Combine all ingredients and pour over cracked-ice-filled glass.

MEDITERRANEAN COOLER

serves 6

4 cups	tomato juice	1 L
1	cucumber, peeled	1
½	green pepper, seeded	½
¼	purple onion, peeled	¼
6	celery sticks	6
6	parsley sprigs	6

Blend tomato juice, cucumber, green pepper and onion in food processor or blender. Pour into ice-filled glasses. Garnish with celery sticks and sprigs of parsley.

VEGETABLE SUPREME

serves 1

1	medium carrot	1
1	celery stick	1
2	tomatoes	2
2	green onions	2
½ cup	water	125 mL
1 tbsp.	Worcestershire sauce	15 mL
2 drops	Tabasco	2 drops
	salt and pepper to taste	
	lime wedge for garnish	

Put all ingredients, except lime wedge, in food processor and blend until smooth. Refrigerate until cold. Serve in cracked-ice-filled glass, garnishing with a lime wedge.

VEGETABLE SENSATION

serves 6-8

8 cups	beef or vegetable stock	2 L
½	celery stalk	½
2	medium carrots	2
3	green onions	3
½ tsp.	thyme	2 mL
4	whole peppercorns	4
¼ tsp.	thyme	1 mL
	salt and pepper to taste	
	celery stick for garnish	
	jumbo prawn for garnish (optional)	

Put all vegetables and spices in food processor and blend until smooth. Set aside. Bring beef stock to a boil; add vegetables and spices and bring to a boil again. Serve hot or cold. If serving cold, garnish with a celery stick and/or a jumbo prawn.

note

If serving cold, be sure to cool to room temperature before storing in refrigerator.

See photograph page 51.

PINEAPPLE - CELERY

spritzer

serves 3-4

2 cups	pineapple chunks, with juice	500 mL
2	celery sticks	2
1	green onion	1
½ tsp.	ground cinnamon	2 mL
½ cup	soda, 7-Up or Sprite	125 mL
	celery stick or pineapple wedge for garnish	

Combine pineapple, celery, onion and cinnamon in food processor. Blend until smooth. Strain and add soda. Serve in ice-filled glasses and garnish with celery stick or pineapple wedge.

GRAPE - RASPBERRY

spritzer

serves 6

2 cups	seedless grapes	500 mL
2 cups	raspberries	500 mL
½ tsp.	cinnamon	2 mL
¼ cup	sugar (optional)	50 mL
2 cups	7-Up, Sprite or soda	500 mL

Combine grapes and raspberries in food processor and purée. Add cinnamon and sugar. Blend well. Add fruit mixture to 7-Up. Pour into cracked-ice-filled glasses.

GINGERED GRAPE

serves 8

4 cups	grape juice	1 L
4 cups	ginger ale	1 L

Combine ingredients and pour into cracked-ice-filled glasses.

OKANAGAN SPRITZER

serves 10-12

1 cup	orange juice	250 mL
3	cinnamon sticks	3
¼ tsp.	ground cloves	1 mL
12 cups	apple cider	3 L
	soda water	
	spiced apple rings	

Bring orange juice, cinnamon sticks and cloves to a boil. Add apple cider and serve in cracked-ice-filled glasses with a dash of soda. Garnish with spiced apple rings.

SEA BREEZE COCKTAIL

serves 8

1	cantaloupe	1
2	bananas	2
3	kiwi	3
1 cup	seedless green grapes	250 mL
1 cup	pineapple chunks	250 mL
4 cups	strawberries	1 L
½ cup	raspberries	125 mL
2 tbsp.	sugar	30 mL
	soda water	
	fruit slices for garnish	

Peel and seed cantaloupe. Peel bananas and kiwi. Blend all ingredients, except soda, until smooth. Pour into ice-filled glasses and top with soda. Stir and serve. Garnish with a slice of fruit of your choice.

CITRUS DELIGHT

serves 4

1	grapefruit, peeled	1
2	navel oranges, peeled	2
½	lime, peeled	½
2	plums, stemmed and pitted	2
2	peaches, halved and pitted	2
¼ tsp.	allspice	1 mL
1 cup	sugar	250 mL
3 cups	water	750 mL
	oranges slices for garnish	

Combine all fruit in a food processor; purée. Add allspice and sugar. Stir in cold water until sugar is dissolved. Serve in tall ice-filled glasses. Garnish with orange slices.

BLUEBERRY CORDIAL

serves 6

1½ cups	sugar	375 mL
2 cups	water	500 mL
1 cup	blueberries, puréed	250 mL

Blend sugar and water until dissolved. Add blueberries and stir until blended. Serve in cracked-ice-filled glasses.

ORANGEADE

serves 8

1 cup	sugar	250 mL
3 cups	water	750 mL
2 tsp.	grated orange rind	10 mL
4 cups	fresh orange juice, strained	1 L
8	cinnamon sticks	8

Blend sugar and water until sugar is dissolved: add orange rind and juice. Stir until well blended. Serve in cracked-ice-filled glasses, garnishing with cinnamon sticks.

PEACHY SMOOTH

serves 4

1 cup	sliced peaches	250 mL
1 cup	half & half	250 mL
⅓ tsp.	almond extract	1.5 mL
2 cups	cold milk	500 mL
	peppermint sticks for garnish	

Blend all ingredients, except peppermint sticks, until smooth. Pour into cracked-ice-filled glasses. Garnish with peppermint sticks.

CHOCOLATE - ORANGE

a creamy float

serves 8-10

2 cups	orange juice	500 mL
2 cups	chocolate ice cream	500 mL
	crushed ice	
4 cups	7-Up or Sprite	1 L
	orange slice for garnish	

Mix orange juice and ice cream until smooth. Fill ¾ of each glass with crushed ice. Half fill glasses with orange-chocolate mixture. Top with 7-Up. Garnish with orange slice.

STRAWBERRY YOGURT

a light cooler

serves 4-6

2½ cups	fresh strawberries	625 mL
1½ cups	natural yogurt	375 mL
1 cup	water	250 mL
1 cup	ice cubes	250 mL

Process all ingredients together in a food processor, until ice is crushed. Pour into tall glasses and serve.

variation

Use any of your favorite fruit. Garnish with a fresh strawberry

B A N A N A   S P L I T

serves 2

4 scoops	vanilla ice cream	4 scoops
2	bananas, peeled, quartered	2
⅛ cup	crushed pineapple	25 mL
¼ cup	fresh strawberries	50 mL
¼ cup	butterscotch topping	50 mL
¼ cup	walnuts	50 mL
	whipped cream & maraschino cherries	

Blend all ingredients, except whipped cream and cherries, until smooth. Pour into tall glasses and top with whipped cream and stemmed maraschino cherries.

P U M P K I N   E G G N O G

serves 4

2 cups	pumpkin	500 mL
1 cup	water	250 mL
¼ cup	milk	50 mL
¾ cup	boiled potatoes	175 mL
2	eggs	2
	salt, pepper, allspice, nutmeg, brown sugar to taste	

Cook pumpkin until soft. Combine all ingredients, except spices, in food processor and blend until smooth. If too thick, add extra cream or milk until desired thickness. Season to taste. This can be served warm or cold.

H O N E Y   C H O C O L A T E   C O W

serves 4

4 cups	milk, your choice	1 L
2	cinnamon sticks	2
¼ cup	cocoa powder	50 mL
⅓ cup	honey	75 mL

Place milk and cinnamon sticks in a saucepan and bring to a boil. Discard cinnamon sticks. Stir in cocoa and return to heat. Stir in honey and serve.

DIPS, SAUCES & RELISHES

T O M A T O   C R E A M

yields ½ cup (125 mL)

2	medium tomatoes	2
1	small onion	1
1	large garlic clove	1
2 tsp.	sweet basil	10 mL
1 tsp.	oregano	5 mL
¼ cup	whipping cream	50 mL
	salt and pepper to taste	

Put coarsely chopped tomato, onion and garlic in food processor; blend until smooth. Place in saucepan and bring to a boil over medium-high heat. Add spices and cream, bring to a boil, stirring constantly until reduced to desired thickness. Adjust seasoning according to taste.

serving suggestions

This sauce is excellent tossed in pasta or as an accompaniment to Carrot and Turnip Timbales, page 66.

C U C U M B E R   S A U C E

yields 1½ cups (375 mL)

1	cucumber, peeled, seeded, finely chopped	1
1 cup	plain yogurt	250 mL
¼ cup	sour cream	50 mL
1	lemon, juice of	1
3 tbsp.	finely chopped chives	45 mL
	salt and pepper to taste	

Combine all ingredients; refrigerate until needed.

serving suggestions

Serve as a sauce with poached or broiled fish or use as a dip with pita bread.

M U S T A R D   S A U C E

yields 1¼ cups (300 mL)

1 cup	whipping cream	250 mL
2 tbsp.	Dijon mustard	30 mL
4 tbsp.	prepared mustard	60 mL
½ cup	chopped green onion	125 mL
¼ tsp.	dry mustard	1 mL

Combine all ingredients in a food processor; blend until smooth. Serve this sauce either hot or cold. To serve hot, simply bring to a boil for 5 minutes and serve.

serving suggestions

A delicious topping for broiled steaks or lamb chops. Garnish with a sprig of fresh rosemary for added appeal.

G I N G E R   M U S T A R D   S A U C E

yields ¾ cup (175 mL)

½ tsp.	dry mustard	2 mL
1½ tsp	ginger	7 mL
1 tsp.	salt	5 mL
½ tsp.	Worcestershire sauce	2 mL
1 tsp.	water	5 mL
½ cup	sour cream	125 mL
¼ tsp.	minced garlic	1 mL

Combine all ingredients in food processor, blending until smooth. This sauce is great with fish, chicken and as a dip for vegetable kebabs.

BLACKBERRY HOLLANDAISE

yields 1½ cups (375 mL)

6	eggs	6
3 tbsp.	cold water	45 mL
2 tsp.	lemon juice	10 mL
	dash of salt	
1¼ cups	clarified butter	300 mL
1 cup	blackberries ¾ cup (175 mL) puréed	250 mL
	¼ cup (50 mL) whole	

Separate eggs; put yolks and water together over a double boiler and heat steadily and evenly. Heat and beat until frothy, then remove from heat. Add lemon juice and salt. While whisking steadily, add clarified butter slowly, so it does not separate. When butter is all incorporated, sauce should thicken. When it is thickened, slowly add puréed blackberries. Blend well. Garnish with whole blackberries.

note

Do not refrigerate. This will not last overnight.

serving suggestions

A new twist for Eggs Benedict instead of regular Hollandaise. Also good with fish and as a dip for raw vegetables.

SPICY HONEY SAUCE

yields 1 cup (250 mL)

⅔ cup	strong chicken or vegetable stock	150 mL
¼ cup	honey	50 mL
2 tsp.	Louisiana hot sauce	10 mL
1 tsp.	grated fresh ginger	5 mL
1 tsp.	cornstarch	5 mL
2 tsp.	cold water	10 mL

SPICY HONEY SAUCE

(continued)

Mix all ingredients together, except cornstarch and water. Put all ingredients in a small saucepan and bring to a boil; add cornstarch mixture and cook until thickened.

serving suggestions

Use as a dip with chicken wings. Serve with broiled tomatoes or with a hot vegetable platter.

KUMQUAT & BRANDY SAUCE

yields 2 cups (500 mL)

1 lb.	kumquats, finely diced	500 g
2 cups	chicken or vegetable stock	500 mL
¼ cup	brandy	50 mL
1 tbsp.	whole black peppercorns	15 mL
2	bay leaves	2
1	medium onion, coarsely chopped	1
2 tbsp.	cranberry sauce	30 mL
1	garlic clove, minced	1
½ cup	brown sugar	125 mL

Combine all ingredients in a medium-sized pot; bring to a hard boil for 10 minutes. Remove bay leaves; boil 20 minutes more. Blend in food processor, then strain. Put mixture into a clean pot; bring to a boil for 18 minutes more, or until it starts to thicken.

serving suggestions

Excellent with game birds and chicken, as well as with pork dishes. This sauce also complements vegetable dishes such as sweet potatoes or braised cabbage.

S P I C Y   C H E E S E   D I P

yields 1½ cups (375 mL)

8 oz.	cream cheese, cut in chunks	250 g
½ cup	sour cream	125 mL
½ tsp.	cayenne pepper	2 mL
	Louisiana hot sauce to taste	
1 tsp.	salt	5 mL
6 oz.	sharp Cheddar cheese, grated	175 g
2 tbsp.	chopped chives or green onions	30 mL

Put cream cheese in food processor and add sour cream; blend until smooth. Add remaining ingredients, except onions; blend thoroughly. Top with onion for garnish. Refrigerate until needed. This dip will keep for 2 weeks in the refrigerator.

serving suggestions

When heated, this dip is excellent with tiger prawns, vegetable kebabs or raw vegetables.

C U C U M B E R   D I L L   D I P

yields 2 cups (500 mL)

2	medium cucumbers	2
1 cup	sour cream	250 mL
2 tbsp.	chopped fresh dill	30 mL
3 tbsp.	chopped green onion	45 mL
½ tsp.	marjoram	2 mL
	salt and pepper to taste	

Peel cucumber and slice in half lengthwise. Take small spoon and scrape out seeds. Finely dice cucumber, add to remaining ingredients, mix well and refrigerate for a minimum of 1 hour.

C H U N K Y   S A L S A

yields 2½ cups (625 mL)

1	cucumber	1
1	onion	1
1	green pepper	1
2	large garlic cloves	2
8	jalapeño peppers, dried (ground up)	8
1¼ cups	crushed tomatoes	300 mL
3 tbsp.	tomato purée	45 mL
1 tbsp.	cumin powder	15
½ tsp.	black pepper	2 mL
2 tbsp.	salt	30 mL
¼ cup	wine vinegar	50 mL
½ cup	vegetable oil	125 mL
2 tbsp.	hot sauce	30 mL
1	cucumber, skinned and finely diced	1
1	green pepper, finely diced	1
1	onion, finely diced	1
⅛ cup	finely chopped parsley	25 mL

Grind up first 5 ingredients. Mix in crushed tomatoes, tomato purée, cumin, pepper, salt, vinegar, oil and hot sauce and set aside. Combine remaining cucumber, green pepper, onion and the parsley and add to tomato mixture. Refrigerate until needed.

serving suggestions

This makes an excellent dip for nachos.

MARINADE FOR VEGETABLES

yields 1 cup (250 mL)

1 cup	brown sugar	250 mL
½ cup	soy sauce	125 mL
1 tbsp.	Worcestershire sauce	15 mL
1	garlic clove, minced	1
2 tsp.	ground ginger	10 mL
	salt and pepper to taste	

Combine all ingredients; bring to a boil for 10 to 15 minutes, or until it starts to thicken. Cool; toss with your choice of vegetables and marinate several hours or overnight before serving. As an alternative, vegetables may be mixed with hot marinade. It will only take a few minutes for the vegetables to absorb the marinade. Serve immediately to prevent the vegetables from becoming soggy.

FRUIT VINAIGRETTE

blackberry, raspberry, peach, orange, etc.

yields 2 cups (500 mL)

1½ cups	melon, or any fresh fruit desired	375 mL
½ cup	cider vinegar	125 mL
1¼ cups	vegetable or grape seed oil	300 mL
1 tbsp.	pink peppercorns	15 mL
½ tsp.	oregano	2 mL
1 tsp.	sugar	5 mL
1 tsp.	minced garlic	5 mL
¼ tsp.	dried sweet basil	1 mL

Combine all ingredients in a blender or food processor and mix until smooth. Pour into a covered container to store until needed. This is an excellent dressing for salads. When serving, garnish with watercress and a piece of the fresh fruit used to make dressing.

variations

To make your favorite fruit vinaigrettes, substitute blackberries, raspberries, peaches, oranges, etc. for melon.

C A E S A R   D R E S S I N G

yields 3 cups (750 mL)

3	large whole eggs	3
½ cup	wine vinegar	125 mL
1½ tbsp.	dry mustard powder	22 mL
2	garlic cloves, minced	2
1½ tbsp.	salt	22 mL
¾ tbsp.	white pepper	12 mL
4½ tbsp.	Worcestershire sauce	67 mL
7½ tbsp.	lemon juice	112 mL
½ cup	wine vinegar	125 mL
7½ tbsp.	grated Parmesan cheese	112 mL
2 cups	vegetable oil	500 mL

Combine first 6 ingredients; mix until smooth, using a blender or food processor if you wish. Add the remaining ingredients, adding oil last. Blend thoroughly until smooth, adding vegetable oil in a slow steady stream to prevent it from separating. Refrigerate until needed. May be refrigerated, in a covered jar, up to 2 weeks.

G R E E N   M A Y O N N A I S E

yields 1½ cups (375 mL)

½ cup	cooked, chopped spinach	125 mL
1 tbsp.	chopped parsley	15 mL
4 tbsp.	chopped chives	60 mL
1 tbsp.	dillweed	15 mL
1 cup	mayonnaise	250 mL
1 tbsp.	lemon juice	15 mL

Combine all ingredients in a food processor; blend until smooth. Refrigerate until needed. May be stored in refrigerator for 2-3 weeks.

serving suggestions

Serve with fish dishes, potato pancakes, sandwiches or wherever you like to use regular mayonnaise.

ZUCCHINI PEPPER RELISH

Iris Roadhouse/Homemaker-Grandmother

yields 6 cups (1.5 L)

This lady has been dazzling our relatives with her culinary talents even before I became a Chef. This relish is fantastic. It's an excellent accompaniment with any dish. One of my favorite uses is with omelettes. Mrs. Iris Roadhouse hails from Maple Ridge, B.C. Thanks, Aunt Iris, for the recipe.

10 cups	finely chopped zucchini	2.5 L
4 cups	finely chopped Spanish onion	2.5 L
4 tbsp.	salt	60 mL
3	green peppers, seeded, finely chopped	3
3	red peppers, seeded, finely chopped	3
2	yellow peppers, seeded, finely chopped	2
2½ cups	white vinegar	625 mL
3 cups	white sugar	750 mL
1 tbsp.	ground turmeric	15 mL
1 tbsp.	celery seed	15 mL
1 tbsp.	ground nutmeg	15 mL
1 tbsp.	mustard powder	15 mL
1½ tbsp.	cornstarch	22 mL

Combine the first 6 ingredients and let stand for 1½ hours. Drain and rinse with cold water. While this is standing, combine the remaining ingredients in a large bowl. After letting the vegetables stand, and having completed the final rinse, combine all ingredients in a 4-quart (4 L) Dutch oven. Simmer* for about 30 - 40 minutes. Pour into jars and seal when cooled.

*simmer — means: to keep just below the boiling point.

note

When using old jars, be sure to sterilize them before using by boiling both the jars and lids.

Spinach Cheesecake, page 76

GREEN TOMATO CHUTNEY

yields 8 cups (2 L)

4 lbs.	green tomatoes, sliced	2 kg
½ cup	salt	125 mL
1 lb.	apples, cored, finely chopped	500 g
5	onions, finely diced	5
1½ cups	brown sugar	375 mL
3 tbsp.	prepared mustard	45 mL
1 tbsp.	ground ginger	15 mL
3 cups	vinegar	750 mL
⅛ tsp.	nutmeg	0.5 mL
4 tbsp.	raisins	60 mL
2 tbsp.	crushed walnuts	30 mL

Put tomatoes in a casserole or roasting pan and pour salt over them. Let stand for 15-24 hours. Pour off liquid; add remaining ingredients and simmer for 3 hours. Taste, adjusting seasoning. Cool. Seal in sterilized jars.

MANGO & APPLE CHUTNEY

yields 4½ cups (1.125 L)

3	apples, seeded, finely chopped	3
4	medium mangos, finely chopped	4
1 cup	port	250 mL
2	large onions, finely chopped	2
1 cup	raisins, finely chopped	250 mL
2 tbsp.	ground ginger	30 mL
1	jalapeño pepper, seeded, finely chopped	1
2½ cups	sugar	625 mL
3 cups	vinegar	750 mL
2 tsp.	mustard seeds	10 mL

Combine all ingredients in a medium-sized saucepan; bring to a boil. Reduce heat and simmer for 2 hours or until thick. When thickened, pour into jars; seal when cool.

P E A C H   C H U T N E Y

yields 4 cups (1 L)

1 tbsp.	vegetable oil	15 mL
1	garlic clove, minced	1
1 tbsp.	finely chopped onion	15 mL
1	red pepper, finely chopped	1
1	green pepper, finely chopped	1
4 cups	pitted, finely chopped peaches	1 L
1 cup	vinegar	250 mL
¾ cup	brown sugar	175 mL

Heat a medium-sized pan; add oil and garlic; sauté for 30 seconds; add remaining ingredients and bring to a boil. Reduce heat to simmer for 45-60 minutes, until thickened. Seal in glass jars.

C O R N   R E L I S H

yields 8 cups (2 L)

2 cups	corn niblets, frozen	500 mL
2½ cups	vinegar	625 mL
¾ cup	brown sugar	175 mL
1	onion, finely chopped	1
1	green pepper, finely chopped	1
1	red pepper, finely chopped or 1 small jar pimientoes, finely chopped	1
1 tbsp.	dry mustard	15 mL
2 tbsp.	prepared mustard	30 mL
2 tbsp.	cornstarch	30 mL

Place corn in a medium-sized saucepan; add 2¼ cups (550 mL) vinegar and the sugar; bring to boil until sugar is dissolved. Add onion and peppers; simmer for 15-20 minutes. Blend mustards and cornstarch; add remaining ¼ cup (50 mL) vinegar. Blend into corn mixture. Bring mixture to a boil until it thickens. Pour into jars and seal when cooled.

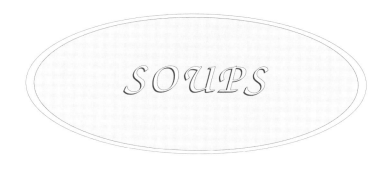

SOUPS

STRAWBERRY MELON SOUP

serves 6

2 cups	strawberries, puréed	500 mL
1 cup	melon meat, watermelon, honeydew or cantaloupe	250 mL
2 tbsp.	finely chopped fresh mint	30 mL
¼ cup	La Grand Passion liqueur	50 mL
1 cup	sparkling wine	250 mL
¼ cup	cold water, if needed	50 mL

Purée strawberries and melon together in food processor or blender; add mint and Grand Passion liqueur slowly while blending. Add wine to desired thickness. If needed, add cold water to dilute it more to your liking.

note

If La Grand Passion liqueur is not available, try your favorite fruit-based liqueur that will complement the flavor of the fruits used.

PEACHES & CHAMPAGNE

chilled

serves 8

3½ cups	sliced fresh peaches or 2 x 14 oz. (398 mL) cans	875 mL
2	mint leaves	2
2 tbsp.	sugar	30 mL
1 tbsp.	cinnamon or allspice	15 mL
2 cups	champagne or sparkling wine mint leaves for garnish	500 mL

Combine peaches with juice in food processor and blend until smooth. Add remaining ingredients, except garnish, blending until smooth. Chill and serve in glass bowls nestled in a bed of cracked ice; garnish with a mint leaf.

G A Z P A C H O

serves 10

5	tomatoes, finely chopped	5
1	green pepper, seeded, finely chopped	1
1	yellow pepper, seeded, finely chopped	1
3	cucumbers, peeled, finely chopped	3
3	garlic cloves, minced	3
2½ cups	V8 juice	625 mL
½ cup	vegetable oil	125 mL
2 tbsp.	red wine vinegar	30 mL
1 tsp.	salt	5 mL
1 tbsp.	lemon juice	15 mL
⅓ tsp.	Tabasco	1.5 mL
3 tsp.	finely minced fresh sweet basil	15 mL
2 tsp.	finely minced oregano leaves	10 mL

Combine all ingredients. Chill overnight. Serve. This soup remains fresh and crunchy for a week in the refrigerator.

variation

Serve with oil and garlic croûtons or julienne of corn tortillas for extra crunch and flavor.

note

All V8 and tomato juices are seasoned, so be careful with additional seasoning when using.

AVOCADO & TOMATO SOUP

chilled

serves 4

2	avocados, peeled & pitted	2
2	tomatoes, finely diced	2
1	cucumber, peeled & finely diced	1
2 cups	V8 juice or tomato juice	500 mL
dash	Worcestershire sauce	dash
¼ tsp.	finely chopped dillweed	1 mL
	salt and pepper to taste	
pinch	crushed cumin	pinch
1	small onion, finely diced	1
	dill sprigs for garnish	
	toast rounds or garlic croûtons	

Purée avocados; stir in tomatoes and cucumber. Add juice and Worcestershire, dill, salt and pepper to taste, cumin and onion. Chill for about 1½ hours before serving. Garnish with a sprig of dill and toast rounds or garlic croûtons.

SUNSET SOUP

chilled

serves 8

2 cups	drained, diced, cooked beets	500 mL
⅓ cup	white sugar	75 mL
¼ cup	cider vinegar	50 mL
½ tsp.	salt	2 mL
2½ cups	cream	625 mL

Prepare beets. Mix sugar, vinegar and salt together until sugar is dissolved; add to cream. Combine with beets and serve cold. Top with a dollop of sour cream and chopped chives.

note

If you would rather have this as a hot soup, simply bring to a boil, and serve immediately.

hot

serves 6

2 tbsp.	butter	30 mL
½	onion, finely diced	½
2 tbsp.	minced garlic	30 mL
3 cups	sliced mushrooms	750 g
4 cups	chicken or vegetable stock	1 L
¾ cup	wild rice, uncooked	175 mL
	salt and white pepper to taste	
¼ cup	brandy (optional)	50 mL

Melt butter in large saucepan. Sauté onions and garlic until lightly done; add mushrooms. Simmer until al dente*. Heat chicken stock to boiling; add wild rice, cover and reduce to simmer. Cook for 45-60 minutes. Just before rice is cooked, add the sautéed onions and mushrooms. Adjust seasoning to taste. For a richer flavor, add ¼ cup (50 mL) of brandy.

variation

This is not a cream soup, but if you wish to make a cream soup just thicken chicken or vegetable stock with a roux or cornstarch before adding mushrooms and onions.

*al dente — Italian phrase meaning "to the tooth", used to describe spaghetti or other pasta at the perfect stage of doneness; tender but with enough firmness to be felt between the teeth.

TOMATO SOUP

serves 8

3 cups	strong chicken or vegetable stock	750 mL
8	tomatoes, medium-sized, puréed	8
1	onion, minced	1
3 tbsp.	tomato paste	45 mL
1 tbsp.	sweet basil	15 mL
1	medium bay leaf	1
	salt and pepper to taste	
dash	Worcestershire sauce	dash
	croûtons for garnish	

Bring chicken stock to a boil; add puréed tomatoes, onion, tomato paste and seasoning. Bring to a boil again. Remove bay leaf and adjust seasoning. Serve with croûtons.

CURRIED TOMATO SOUP

serves 8

2	celery stalks, sliced	2
1	green pepper, seeded, diced	1
5 cups	tomatoes, stewed or crushed	1.25 L
1	onion, peeled, sliced	1
1	carrot, peeled, sliced	1
2 tbsp.	curry powder	30 mL
¼ cup	whipping cream	50 mL
4 cups	chicken or vegetable stock	1 L
	salt and pepper to taste	

Combine all ingredients, except cream, stock, salt and pepper, in food processor. Blend until smooth; add cream. Continue blending until well combined. Put processed mixture and stock in soup pot and bring to a boil. Adjust salt and pepper according to taste. Serve with breadsticks.

G R A N D   O N I O N   S O U P

serves 6

4	medium onions, peeled, sliced	4
2 tbsp.	butter	30 mL
1 tbsp.	thyme	15 mL
2½ cups	water or chicken stock	625 mL
¼ tsp.	ground ginger	1 mL
	salt and pepper to taste	
2 tbsp.	grated Parmesan cheese	30 mL
½ cup	Grand Marnier	125 mL
	croûtons for garnish	

Sauté onion in butter until well browned; add thyme when onions are browned. Add water; bring to a boil; add ginger, salt and pepper and Parmesan cheese. Taste and adjust seasoning. Just before serving, add Grand Marnier. Keep hot. Serve with croûtons.

croûtons

1	French stick, sliced ½″ (1.2 cm) and buttered, about 12 slices	1
1 tbsp.	grated Parmesan cheese	15 mL
3 tbsp.	grated mozzarella cheese	45 mL
3 tbsp.	grated Swiss cheese	45 mL

Lay sliced and buttered bread on cookie sheet; top with Parmesan, mozzarella and Swiss cheeses. Bake bread slices in oven until cheese is melted. Serve croûtons on the side or place on top of soup.

O N I O N   S O U P

serves 6

4 tbsp.	butter	60 mL
5	onions, sliced	5
1	celery stalk, sliced	1
4 cups	beef stock	1 L
2	large potatoes, peeled, finely diced	2
1½ cups	dry white wine	375 mL
2 tbsp.	cornstarch	30 mL
½ cup	whipping cream	125 mL
	salt and pepper to taste	

Melt butter; sauté onion and celery until soft. Add beef stock, potatoes and wine; bring to a boil. Combine cornstarch and whipping cream. Add mixture to soup, mixing briskly to avoid lumpiness. Bring to a boil. Add salt and pepper to taste.

M I N T E D   S P I N A C H   S O U P

serves 6

2 tbsp.	butter	30 mL
2	medium-sized onions, finely diced	2
2 cups	cleaned, chopped spinach	500 mL
1½ cups	chicken or vegetable stock	375 mL
½ cup	peas	125 mL
¾ cup	whipping cream	175 mL
1 cup	cleaned, finely chopped fresh mint	250 mL
	salt and pepper to taste	

Melt butter in large saucepan. Sauté onions until tender. Add spinach, bouillon, peas and whipping cream, and simmer for 20 minutes. Put simmered ingredients in food processor and blend until smooth. Add mint and blend again. Put all ingredients back on the stove and bring to a boil for 5 minutes. Add salt and pepper to taste. Serve.

POTATO CHERVIL SOUP

serves 6

3	medium potatoes	3
1 tbsp.	butter	15 mL
2	leeks, finely diced	2
2½ cups	chicken stock or potato water	625 mL
1¾ tbsp.	chervil, finely chopped	25 mL
	salt and white pepper, to taste	

Peel potatoes, and cook until soft, but not mushy; purée. Melt butter in 2-quart (2 L) Dutch oven; sauté leeks, add stock and puréed potatoes. Bring to a boil; add chervil and adjust seasonings. Serve with cheese sticks.

variations

Add ½ cup (125 mL) finely diced Italian hot sausage or roasted lamb. Add ¾ cup (175 mL) shredded Swiss cheese. Add almost anything. Use your imagination.

CHEESE CARROT SOUP

three cheese flavors

serves 8

2½ cups	chicken or vegetable stock or water or 1¼ cups (300 mL) each water and tomato juice	625 mL
4	large carrots, peeled, puréed	4
1	large onion, peeled, puréed	1
1	bay leaf	1
	salt and pepper to taste	
3 tbsp.	cold water	45 mL
2 tbsp.	cornstarch	30 mL
¼ cup	finely chopped Italian parsley	50 mL
½ cup	grated medium Cheddar cheese	125 mL
½ cup	grated Gouda cheese	125 mL
¼ cup	grated Provolone cheese	50 mL

Bring stock to a boil; add puréed carrots, onion, bay leaf, salt and pepper; Bring to a boil again. Adjust seasoning, thicken soup with water and cornstarch; bring to a boil and hold hot. Remove bay leaf. Just before serving, add parsley and stir; add grated cheeses and serve with toasted English muffins.

CAJUN CORN & RED PEPPER

chowder

serves 4

1	fresh jalapeño pepper, seeded, finely sliced	1
½ cup	finely diced white onion	125 mL
3 tbsp.	butter	45 mL
1½ cups	corn niblets	375 mL
3	garlic cloves, minced*	3
2½ cups	milk	625 mL
	salt and pepper to taste	
dash	of your favorite hot sauce (optional)	dash
1	red bell pepper, halved, seeded, finely sliced	1

Slice jalapeño pepper, remove seeds, and finely slice. Place in a bowl with about 2 cups (500 mL) of water, and let soak. Chop the onion. Place butter, onion and drained jalapeño pepper into a 3-quart (3 L) saucepan, and sauté*. Prepare corn. If fresh, cut the kernels off the cob. Add corn and garlic to the onion mixture, and sauté for about 5 minutes. Add the milk. Bring to a boil, turn heat to low, and simmer for about 10-15 minutes. Remove from heat, strain and place liquid back in pot. Put vegetable mixture into food processor or blender and purée*. Add to the liquid, reheat and adjust seasonings. Garnish with the sliced red pepper. Serve with corn chips. For a change, top with a little of your favorite shredded cheese.

*mince – means to chop very finely, but not to purée.
*sauté – means to fry over high heat with a little amount of fat.
*purée – means to grind or process to a smooth pulp.

P A S S I O N & P U M P K I N

delicious taste & velvet texture

serves 4

4 cups	milk or cream	1 L
½ cup	finely diced onion	125 mL
1	small bay leaf	1
3 tbsp.	butter	45 mL
3 tbsp.	flour	45 mL
2½ cups	puréed pumpkin	625 mL
1 tsp.	salt	5 mL
¼ tsp.	celery salt	1 mL
dash	allspice	dash
dash	cayenne pepper	dash
¼ cup	**La Grande Passion liqueur**	50 mL

Scald* milk, onion and bay leaf in a 3-quart (3 L) Dutch oven. Remove bay leaf and set milk aside in a bowl. In the same pot, melt butter and mix in flour to make a roux*. Cook about 2 minutes, slowly adding the milk mixture and stirring constantly. Stir in the puréed pumpkin. Add the spices; bring to a boil. Reduce heat and simmer for about 10 minutes, or until thickened. Adjust seasonings. Add La Grand Passion liqueur. Simmer for 6 more minutes before serving. This soup is fantastic with Cheddar cheese bread sticks.

*scald - means to heat but not to point of boiling
*roux - means mix equal amounts of fat and flour for the purpose of thickening.
        The proper consistency is like wet sand.

note

If La Grande Passion liqueur is not available use brandy, Cognac or Armagnac.

V E G E T A B L E   C H O W D E R

serves 6

3 cups	diced potatoes	750 mL
1 cup	diced carrots	250 mL
	chicken or vegetable stock or water	
3 tbsp.	vegetable oil	45 mL
½ cup	diced onion	125 mL
1	yellow or orange pepper, diced	1
1 cup	diced green beans	250 mL
2 tbsp.	flour	30 mL
2 cups	milk	500 mL
2 cups	crushed tomatoes	500 mL
	salt and pepper to taste	

Cover potatoes and carrots with chicken stock or water and cook until tender. In a saucepan, heat oil and sauté onion, yellow pepper and green beans until al dente. Add flour and blend in; add milk and cook until smooth. Add remaining ingredients to potato and carrot mixture. Add flour mixture, stirring constantly until combined.

M I N E S T R O N E   S O U P

serves 10

pesto

6 tbsp.	olive oil	90 mL
5 tbsp.	celery leaves	75 mL
5 tbsp.	parsley	75 mL
¼ tsp.	rosemary	1 mL
¼ tsp.	sweet basil	1 mL
¼ tsp.	marjoram	1 mL
¼ tsp.	oregano	1 mL
¼ tsp.	thyme	1 mL
¾ cup	chopped onions	175 mL
½ cup	chopped celery	125 mL
½ cup	chopped carrots	125 mL
¼ cup	chopped green peppers	50 mL
¼ cup	chopped cabbage or spinach	50 mL
1	garlic clove, crushed	1
8 cups	chicken or vegetable stock	2 L
1 cup	stewed tomatoes, crushed	250 mL
3 tbsp.	ditalini or other macaroni product	45 mL
½ cup	chick-peas	125 mL
3 tbsp.	blackeyed beans or other dried beans, cooked	45 mL
	salt and pepper to taste	

Combine all Pesto ingredients in a food processor or blender. Put Pesto into soup pot. Add onions, celery, carrots, green peppers, cabbage and garlic to soup pot and sauté. Add stock and tomato; simmer for about 8-10 minutes. Add ditalini to soup and cook until done, about 10 minutes. Add chick-peas and cooked beans; adjust seasoning.

JULIENNE OF VEGETABLE

Cajun-style soup

serves 6

2 tbsp.	butter or margarine	30 mL
¼ cup	julienne of purple onion	50 mL
¼ cup	julienne of carrot	50 mL
¼ cup	julienne of potato	50 mL
¼ cup	julienne of green bell pepper	50 mL
¼ cup	julienne of red bell pepper	50 mL
¼ cup	julienne of yellow bell pepper	50 mL
¼ cup	julienne of celery	50 mL
6 cups	beef or vegetable stock	1.5 L
5	garlic cloves, minced	5
1 tsp.	paprika	5 mL
1 tsp.	ground black pepper	5 mL
2 tsp.	oregano	10 mL
1 tsp.	ground cumin	5 mL
½ tsp.	celery seed	2 mL
1	bay leaf	1
1½ tsp.	thyme	7 mL
	salt and pepper to taste	
3	tomatoes, puréed	3
1 cup	cooked blackeyed peas	250 mL
2	hot cherry peppers, seeded, finely sliced	2

Heat butter in a 4-quart (4 L) saucepan. Add onion, carrot, potato, peppers and celery; sauté for about 10 minutes. Add beef stock, spices and puréed tomatoes and bring to a boil. Taste and adjust seasoning with the salt and pepper. Add blackeyed peas and sliced cherry peppers; simmer for about 10 minutes, and serve. Great with mango and apple chutney, page 35, and multi-grain dinner rolls.

See photograph on opposite page.

Julienne of Vegetable Soup, page 50
Vegetable Sensation, page 17

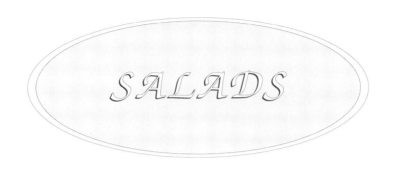

SALADS

S U M M E R   S A L A D

with honey yogurt dressing

serves 4

1 bunch	green onions, diced	1 bunch
1 cup	shredded carrot	250 mL
12	radishes, sliced	12
1 cup	finely diced celery	250 mL
1 cup	cleaned, chopped watercress	250 mL
1	cucumber, thinly sliced	1
1 cup	chopped pecans	250 mL

Toss all ingredients together and top with Honey Yogurt Dressing.

honey yogurt dressing

1 cup	yogurt	250 mL
1 tbsp.	lemon juice	15 mL
4 tbsp.	honey	60 mL

Combine all ingredients. Blend well and use as a dressing.

A S P A R A G U S   P E C A N   S A L A D

with blackberry vinaigrette

serves 6

1 head	romaine or assorted lettuce	1 head
1 bunch	asparagus	1 bunch
1 cup	pecans	250 mL
½ cup	diced green onion	125 mL
¼ cup	diced celery	50 mL
	whole blackberries and	
	watercress sprigs for garnish	

ASPARAGUS PECAN SALAD

(continued)

Clean romaine and cut into bite-sized pieces. Blanche asparagus, and cut into thirds. Prepare 6 salad plates with beds of romaine lettuce. Toss remaining ingredients together and place on top of romaine beds. Prepare Blackberry or Raspberry Vinaigrette, page 30, and drizzle over salads. Garnish each with a few berries and a watercress sprig.

See photograph on front cover.

CELERY & PEPPER SALAD

with orange dressing

serves 2

2	celery stalks, cleaned and finely sliced	2
1	green pepper, cleaned and finely sliced	1
1	red pepper, cleaned and finely sliced	1
1	yellow pepper, cleaned and finely sliced	1
4	green onions, cleaned and diced	4

Combine all ingredients and toss. Top with Orange Dressing, as follows.

orange dressing

⅓ cup	fresh orange juice	75 mL
1½ tsp.	grated orange rind	7 mL
1 tbsp.	Triple Sec	15 mL
1 tbsp.	vegetable oil	15 mL
½ tsp.	sugar	2 mL

Combine all ingredients.

CUCUMBER SALAD

with peanut dressing

serves 8

2	large cucumbers, washed and thinly sliced	2
1	large carrot, washed and sliced	1
2	broccoli stalks, washed, cut into small sprigs	2

Combine all ingredients and toss. Top with Peanut Dressing, as follows.

peanut dressing

2 tbsp.	chunky-style peanut butter	30 mL
½ cup	whipping cream	125 mL
½ cup	mayonnaise	125 mL
¼ cup	chopped green onions	50 mL

Combine all ingredients.

CUCUMBER & APPLE SALAD

serves 4

½ cup	raisins	125 mL
2	medium cucumbers, peeled, thinly sliced	2
6	radishes, washed, sliced	6
2	apples, cored, sliced	2
1 cup	sour cream	175 mL
2 tbsp.	lemon juice	30 mL
1 tbsp.	chopped watercress or parsley	15 mL
1 tbsp.	black pepper	15 mL
	salt and pepper to taste	

Place raisins in warm water to plump; drain. Combine all ingredients; toss until blended. Chill before serving.

CUCUMBER ORANGE SALAD

with orange vinaigrette dressing

serves 6-8

3 cups	cucumber, peeled, diced	750 mL
3	oranges, peeled, sliced	3
½ cup	diced green onions	125 mL
¼ cup	diced yellow pepper	50 mL

Combine and toss all ingredients. Prepare Orange Vinaigrette Dressing, page 30. Serve this salad chilled. Add dressing just before serving.

MANDARIN ORANGE SALAD

with yogurt and triple sec dressing

serves 6

1 head	butterleaf lettuce	1
6 tbsp.	sliced almonds for garnish	90 mL

Clean lettuce and tear into bite-sized pieces. Place in a bowl in the crisper of the refrigerator for 10-12 minutes, for firmness. Place lettuce on salad plates; top with Yogurt and Triple Sec Dressing, as follows.

yogurt and triple sec dressing

6 tbsp.	yogurt, plain or orange-flavored	90 mL
6 oz.	can mandarin oranges	170 mL
3 tbsp.	Triple Sec liqueur	45 mL

Combine yogurt and mandarin oranges, including the juice. Add Triple Sec.

SALAD ANTONIO SUPREME

with peach vinaigrette

serves 2

1 bunch	watercress	1 bunch
¼ head	romaine lettuce, cut into bite-sized pieces	¼ head
¼ bag	spinach	¼ bag
1 oz.	Gouda cheese, cut julienne	30 g
1 oz.	Cheddar cheese, cut julienne	30 g
1 oz.	Edam cheese, cut julienne	30 g
1	tomato, quartered	1
1	kiwifruit, peeled and quartered	1
4	cucumber slices	4
2	onion slices, ¼" thick	2
2	green or yellow pepper rings	2
2	papaya slices, peeled	2
1	hard-boiled egg, peeled, sliced	1
	Peach Vinaigrette, page 30	

Combine watercress, romaine and spinach. Place on a plate or in a bowl. Arrange the remaining ingredients on top of the lettuce mixture. Top salad with Peach Vinaigrette.

PEACH & CARROT SALAD

with peach vinaigrette

serves 10

1 cup	peach juice	250 mL
½	lemon, juice of	½
⅛ tsp.	salt	0.5 mL
1 tbsp.	sugar	15 mL
½ cup	raisins	125 mL
3	peaches, fresh, pitted, sliced	3
4	carrots, peeled, shredded	4
1½ heads	lettuce, cleaned	1½ heads
	fresh mint for garnish	
	Peach Vinaigrette, page 30	

PEACH & CARROT SALAD

(continued)

Combine peach juice, lemon juice, salt, sugar and raisins; boil about 5 minutes, until raisins plump up; remove from heat, drain and cool. Combine raisins, peaches and shredded carrots; toss with Peach Vinaigrette. Arrange beds of lettuce on 10 salad plates. Place ½ cup (125 mL) of peach mixture on each bed of lettuce. Garnish with fresh mint.

HAWAIIAN WALDORF SALAD

serves 8

1 head	lettuce	1
2½ cups	apples, peeled, cored, sliced	625 mL
3	celery stalks, sliced	3
1 cup	mayonnaise	250 mL
2 tbsp.	lemon juice	30 mL
2	bananas, peeled, sliced	2
½ cup	halved or crushed pecans	125 mL
6 tbsp.	coconut milk	90 mL
½ tsp.	allspice	2 mL
3 tbsp.	freshly grated coconut	45 mL
	mint leaves for garnish	

Clean lettuce; make 8 beds on individual salad plates. Combine all remaining ingredients, except grated coconut and mint leaves. Divide between the 8 beds of lettuce, top with grated coconut and garnish with a mint leaf.

PINEAPPLE & PEPPER SLAW

serves 6

1	red pepper, seeded, finely sliced	1
1	green pepper, seeded, finely sliced	1
1	yellow pepper, seeded, finely sliced	1
1 cup	pineapple chunks	250 mL
1 tsp.	dry mustard	5 mL
1 tsp.	lemon juice	5 mL
1½ cups	mayonnaise	375 mL
1 tbsp.	sugar	15 mL

Combine all ingredients; refrigerate overnight before serving.

ARTICHOKES & TOMATOES

serves 8

1 cup	canned or bottled artichoke hearts	250 mL
½ cup	white wine	125 mL
1	lemon, juice of	1
1 cup	celery, finely diced	250 mL
6	tomatoes, sliced	6
2	onions, finely diced	2
1	garlic clove, minced	1
½ cup	beef broth	125 mL
½ tsp.	sweet basil	2 mL
½ tsp.	oregano	2 mL
	salt and pepper to taste	

Drain artichoke hearts and slice in half. Combine artichokes with the rest of the ingredients; toss and marinate in refrigerator for 8 hours before serving.

B A B Y   C O R N   S A L A D

serves 6

½ cup	finely chopped onion	125 mL
½ cup	finely diced green pepper	125 mL
5 tbsp.	chopped pimiento	75 mL
3 tbsp.	sugar	45 mL
½ tsp.	salt	2 mL
½ tsp.	celery salt	2 mL
½ tsp.	dry mustard	2 mL
½ cup	cider vinegar	125 mL
½ cup	water	125 mL
3 cups	white baby corn niblets	750 mL
	assorted lettuce	

Combine all ingredients, except corn and lettuce. Bring to a boil; lower heat, cover and simmer for 10 minutes. Add corn; bring to a boil again. Cool to room temperature. Refrigerate until chilled. Serve on beds of lettuce on individual salad plates.

A N T O N I O ' S   B E A N   S A L A D
with fruit vinaigrette

serves 8-10

1 cup	green beans, cooked, cooled, diced	250 mL
1 cup	yellow or wax beans, cooked, cooled, diced	250 mL
1 cup	kidney beans	250 mL
1 cup	chick-peas	250 mL
1 cup	lima beans	250 mL
½ cup	green beans, French-style, cooked	125 mL
½ cup	diced orange pepper	125 mL
½ cup	diced red pepper	125 mL
½ cup	diced green onions	125 mL
⅛ cup	seeded, diced jalapeño peppers	25 mL
½	star fruit (Carambala), diced	½ cup
	Fruit Vinaigrette, page 30	

Combine all ingredients and toss with Fruit Vinaigrette.

POTATO SALAD
traditional, with variations

serves 6-8

3 cups	cooked, diced potatoes	750 mL
½ cup	finely diced onion	125 mL
¼ cup	finely diced celery	50 mL
4	hard-boiled eggs, sliced	4
¼ cup	shredded carrots	50 mL
½ cup	finely diced green pepper	125 mL
¼ cup	prepared mustard*	50 mL
1 cup	mayonnaise*	250 mL
	salt and pepper to taste	

Combine all ingredients except mustard, mayonnaise, salt and pepper; toss gently. Combine mustard, mayonnaise, salt and pepper in a small bowl. Add to potato mixture and toss gently until thoroughly combined. Chill until ready to serve.
*Try the following variations instead of the mustard and mayonnaise.

1. pineapple yogurt & sour cream dressing

½ cup	pineapple yogurt	125 mL
½ cup	sour cream	125 mL
½ tsp.	chopped fresh dillweed	2 mL
¼ cup	chopped green onions	50 mL
½	lime, juice of	½

Combine all ingredients. For a real change use the juice of half an orange.

2. hot raspberry vinaigrette

¼ cup	white vinegar	50 mL
2 cups	fresh raspberries* (save some for garnish)	500 mL
¼ cup	chopped green onion	50 mL
2 tbsp.	chopped fresh parsley	30 mL
1 tsp.	chopped fresh chervil	5 mL
¾ cup	grapeseed oil	175 mL
	roasted pine nuts for garnish	
	mint leaves for garnish	

Combine vinegar, raspberries, green onion, parsley and chervil. Place in a food processor or blender and blend until smooth. Set aside. Heat oil until warm, but not too hot. Mix the potato salad with the vinaigrette; mix in the hot oil and garnish the salad with the reserved berries. Sprinkle with pine nuts, fresh mint and raspberries.
*Reserve ½ cup (125 mL) whole raspberries for garnish.

SIDE & MAIN DISHES

M I N T E D   P E A S

serves 4-6

2 cups	frozen peas	500 mL
1½ tsp.	chopped fresh mint	7 mL
1½ tsp.	sugar	7 mL
3 cups	water	750 mL
1 tbsp.	butter	15 mL
	salt and pepper to taste	

Combine peas, mint and sugar in a saucepan with water; bring to a boil and cover for 5-8 minutes. Drain, add butter, salt and pepper to taste; serve.

P E A S   I N   R U M

with mushrooms & pearl onions

serves 6-8

¼ cup	butter	50 mL
2 cups	small whole mushrooms	500 mL
1 cup	pearl onions	250 mL
4 cups	peas	1 L
¼ cup	finely chopped chives	50 mL
1 tsp.	cinnamon	5 mL
	salt and pepper to taste	
¼ cup	rum	50 mL

Heat large saucepan to melt butter; sauté mushrooms until half cooked; add onions, peas and chives; cook until water has evaporated. Add cinnamon, salt and pepper. Just before serving, add rum and set ablaze. Serve at once.

B R O W N   B E A N S   &   P E A C H E S

serves 10-12

4 cups	white pea beans or navy beans	1 L
1 cup	finely chopped onion	250 mL
1 cup	finely chopped celery	250 mL
3	garlic cloves, minced	3
½ cup	butter	125 mL
2 cups	strong beef or vegetable stock	500 mL
⅓ cup	molasses	75 mL
¾ cup	brown sugar	175 mL
⅓ cup	cider vinegar	75 mL
2 cups	chopped fresh peaches	500 mL

Wash beans; drain; soak overnight in 8 cups (2 L) of water. Sauté onion, celery and garlic in butter on medium heat until tender; add beans, with soaking water; add 2 cups stock. Bring to a boil; reduce heat and simmer for 1 hour. Add the rest of the ingredients, except for peaches. Simmer for 1½ hours or until mixture begins to thicken. After it thickens, remove from heat and add peaches.

note:

Make this dish a day before serving. To reheat, place in 350°F (180°C) oven, in ovenproof dish, and serve when heated through, about 30-45 minutes.

C A L I F O R N I A   O N I O N S

serves 8

4 cups	beef or vegetable stock	1 L
1 tbsp.	brown sugar	15 mL
½ cup	raisins	125 mL
4 cups	pearl onions	1 L
2 tbsp.	cornstarch	30 mL
3 tbsp.	chopped parsley	45 mL

Put stock in an ovenproof dish, reserving ½ cup (125 mL) for mixing with cornstarch later. Mix sugar, raisins and onions with stock and bake at 325°F (160°C) for 2 hours. Remove from oven and add cornstarch/stock mixture. Return to the oven and cook until thickened, about 15 minutes. Before serving, sprinkle with chopped parsley.

S P I N A C H   B A L L S

with mustard sauce

serves 4-6

¼ cup	butter	50 mL
1	medium onion, finely chopped	1
1 bunch	fresh spinach, cleaned and chopped	1 bunch
⅛ tsp.	pepper	0.5 mL
¼ tsp.	sage	1 mL
¼ tsp.	thyme	3 mL
3 cups	fine bread crumbs	750 mL
⅔ cup	Parmesan cheese	150 mL
2	eggs	2
	mustard sauce, page 25	

Melt butter in a small frying pan; sauté onion and spinach. Remove from heat; add remaining ingredients and form into balls. Place on an ungreased baking sheet; bake at 350°F (180°C) for 15 minutes. Serve with Mustard sauce.

C A R R O T S   &   T U R N I P S

timbales

serves 4

1 cup	mashed carrots	250 mL
1 cup	mashed turnips	250 mL
2	large eggs	2
¼ cup	milk or cream	50 mL
1 tbsp.	grated orange rind	15 mL
1 tsp.	nutmeg	5 mL
1 tbsp.	brown sugar	15 mL
	salt and pepper to taste	

Combine all ingredients in a food processor; blend until smooth. Pour into 4, 6 oz. (170 mL) custard cups. Bake in a water bath* at 350°F (180°C).

*To bake in a water bath, stand custard cups in a baking pan; pour hot water into pan to a depth of 1" (2.5 cm).

MAPLE-GLAZED CARROTS

serves 6

2 cups	carrots, peeled, cut into 1" (2.5 cm) pieces	500 g
1 cup	maple syrup (not imitation)	250 mL
¼ cup	butter	50 mL
⅛ cup	chopped parsley	25 mL

Boil carrots until tender; drain. Bring maple syrup and butter to a boil; add carrots. Just before serving, sprinkle chopped parsley on top.

SWEET AND SOUR YAMS

serves 8

2 cups	peeled and chopped yams	500 mL
2½ cups	crushed pineapple	625 mL
3 tbsp.	lemon juice	45 mL
1 tbsp.	cornstarch	15 mL
¼ tsp.	salt	1 mL
1 tbsp.	butter	15 mL
3	green onions, diced	3
½ cup	sliced celery	125 mL
1	green pepper, diced	1

Boil yams until soft. Drain pineapple, reserving syrup. Combine cornstarch with reserved syrup and salt; put into saucepan and bring to a boil; stir in lemon juice. Toss pineapple and yams together in an ovenproof pan; pour sauce over and bake in a 350°F (180°C) oven for 30 minutes. While this is baking, melt butter in a small frying pan, sauté green onions, celery and green pepper until tender. Stir into yam mixture at the end of 30 minutes and serve at once.

B A K E D   P O T A T O E S

extravagant variations

serves 4

Over the years of making stuffed potatoes, I have come across various styles and types. With a little imagination, I have come up with a few variations that might, NO, will open your eyes as to what can be done with a little creativity.

REMEMBER, when removing potato meat, save shells to be refilled.

1. the supreme one

4	baked potatoes	4
¼ cup	fresh green onions, chopped	50 mL
1 cup	sharp Cheddar cheese, grated	250 mL
½ cup	shredded carrot	125 mL
1	large egg	1
¼ cup	sour cream	50 mL
	fresh nutmeg	

Slice off ⅛ of each potato lengthwise. Remove the potato meat and combine with the onions, cheese, carrot, egg and sour cream. Mix together and place back into the potato shells. Grate some fresh nutmeg over top of potato, and place on baking sheet. Bake at 350°F (180°C) for about 10-15 minutes, or until browned.

2. the rolling hills of switzerland

4	baked potatoes	4
½ cup	small broccoli florets	125 mL
¼ cup	finely diced purple onion	50 mL
¾ cup	shredded Swiss cheese	175 mL
¼ cup	finely diced red bell pepper	50 mL
2	large eggs	2

Slice off ⅛ of each potato lengthwise and remove potato meat. Combine with the remaining ingredients. Mix together and stuff back into the potato shells. Place potatoes on a baking sheet. Bake at 350°F (180°C) until browned, about 10-15 minutes. Serve at once.

Pasta Primavera, page 96
with Spinach Pasta, page 92
and Tomato Herb Pasta, page 93

3. the godfather spud

4	baked potatoes	4
⅛ cup	finely diced green bell pepper	25 mL
6	ripe tomatoes, finely minced or puréed	6
¼ cup	finely diced white onion	50 mL
1 tbsp.	fresh chopped oregano	15 mL
1 tbsp.	fresh chopped sweet basil	15 mL
¾ cup	shredded mozzarella	175 mL
2	eggs	2
¼ cup	grated Parmesan cheese	50 mL

Slice off ⅛ of each potato lengthwise and remove potato meat. Sauté all the vegetables and spices. Combine with remaining ingredients and mix in potato meat. Stuff back into the potato shells. Place on baking sheet and bake at 350°F (180°F) until brown, about 15-20 minutes. Serve at once.

4. the dutch apple surprise

4	baked potatoes	4
½ cup	peeled apples, finely diced	125 mL
¼ cup	sour cream	50 mL
¼ cup	brown sugar	50 mL
1 tsp.	allspice	5 mL
	dash of vanilla extract	
1 cup	ground Ritz crackers	250 mL
¾ cup	shredded Cheddar cheese	175 mL
2 tbsp.	melted butter	30 mL
	spiced apple rings for garnish	

Slice off ⅛ of each potato lengthwise and remove potato meat. Combine with the apples, sour cream, sugar, allspice and vanilla. Fill the potato shells with the apple mixture and set aside. Prepare topping by combining crackers, cheese and butter. Place on top of stuffed potatoes. Bake at 350°F (180°C) until browned, about 15-20 minutes. Serve at once. Garnish these extraordinary spuds with spiced apple rings.

STUFFED GREEN PEPPERS

serves 4

3 tbsp.	butter or margarine	45 mL
1	small onion, finely diced	1
¼ cup	sliced mushrooms	250 mL
½ cup	finely chopped raw spinach	125 mL
1	garlic clove, minced	1
¼ cup	tomato paste	50 mL
1 cup	crushed tomatoes	250 mL
1	small garlic clove, minced	1
1 tsp.	sweet basil	5 mL
1 tsp.	oregano	5 mL
1 tbsp.	Parmesan cheese	30 mL
3 cups	cooked rice	750 mL
4	green peppers	4
4	mozzarella cheese slices, ¼" (1 cm) thick	4

In a medium-sized frying pan, melt butter; sauté onion and mushrooms until tender. Add spinach, garlic, tomato paste and crushed tomatoes; bring to a boil. Add spices and Parmesan cheese; mix in rice. Cut off top of green peppers and take out seeds. Fill each pepper with rice mixture and top with a mozzarella cheese slice. Bake at 400°F (200°C) for 20 minutes, or until cheese is golden brown.

CABBAGE ROLLS

serves 6-8

1	medium cabbage, cored	1
4 cups	water	1 L
2 cups	rice	500 mL
1	medium onion, finely chopped	1
1 tsp.	salt	5 mL
½ tsp.	pepper	2 mL
4 tbsp.	butter or margarine	60 mL
1½ cups	V8 juice	375 mL

C A B B A G E   R O L L S

(continued)

Boil cabbage until leaves peel off easily. Combine water, rice and onions in a medium-sized saucepan. Cook rice with seasonings until all the water is gone, about 20 minutes. Cool rice; roll into cabbage leaves, folding sides in as you roll. Butter the sides and bottom of an 8" x 8" (20 cm x 20 cm) ovenproof dish, and place cabbage rolls in dish until all are stacked. Dot top with butter; pour V8 juice over cabbage rolls; cover and place in a 350°F (180°C) oven for 1½-2hours.

wine selection

Valpolicella

Z U C C H I N I   A N D   E G G P L A N T

sauté

serves 6

1 tbsp.	olive oil	15 mL
1 tbsp.	minced garlic	15 mL
2	medium-sized zucchini, diced	2
1	large eggplant, diced	1
3	celery stalks, diced	3
1	medium onion, diced	1
1 cup	tomato purée or 4 tomatoes puréed in food processor	250 mL
1 tbsp.	sweet basil	15 mL
	salt and pepper to taste	
3 cups	hot cooked rice	750 mL

Heat olive oil in saucepan; add garlic. Add zucchini, eggplant, celery and onion and sauté until tender. Add tomato purée and spices; sauté until thoroughly heated. Serve on top of steamed rice.

HOT VEGETABLE PLATTER

with broiled tomatoes

serves 1 as a main course

1	medium tomato,	1
1½ tbsp.	grated Cheddar cheese	22 mL
3 tbsp.	bread crumbs	45 mL
1 tbsp.	Parmesan cheese	15 mL
½ tsp.	rosemary	2 mL
	salt and pepper to taste	
2	large broccoli florets	2
¼ head	cauliflower	¼ head
½ cup	sliced carrots	125 mL
½ cup	green beans	125 mL
2 tbsp.	diced onion	30 mL
7	whole mushrooms	7
½	lemon, juice of	½
	lemon, lime and orange wedges for garnish	
	parsley for garnish	

Cut tomato in half, crown-style*, with a paring knife. Mix together Cheddar cheese, bread crumbs, Parmesan cheese, rosemary, salt and pepper. Top tomatoes with cheese mixture and broil until browned. Blanch broccoli, cauliflower, carrots and green beans, keeping all the vegetables separate and hot. Sauté onions; add mushrooms and sauté until tender. Squeeze fresh lemon juice over mushroom mixture; add salt and pepper to taste. Arrange vegetables on a platter and serve hot with lemon, lime and orange wedges. Garnish with parsley.

*crown-style — means: cut in sharp points by inserting paring knife into tomato at a 45° angle, halfway up the tomato, around the circumference. Pull tomato apart to get 2 equal-sized crowns.

P A C I F I C   S T I R - F R Y

2 tbsp.	vegetable oil	30 mL
3	garlic cloves, minced	3
1 tsp.	grated ginger root	5 mL
½ cup	finely sliced carrot	125 mL
¼ cup	cauliflower florets	50 mL
¼ cup	broccoli florets	50 mL
1 cup	fresh pea pods	250 mL
1 cup	chopped bok choy	250 mL
1 cup	sou choy	250 mL
1 cup	fresh bean sprouts	250 mL
¾ cup	oysters or mushrooms	175 mL
½ cup	chicken broth	125 mL
2 tbsp.	cornstarch	30 mL
1 oz.	dark soy sauce	30 g
1 tbsp.	roasted pine nuts	30 mL

Heat wok or large pot to high; keep on high heat as this dish is cooked very quickly. When hot, add oil, garlic and ginger; fry about 20 seconds. Add vegetables from hardest to softest, at 2 minute intervals, and fast-fry, until all vegetables are combined. Mix the chicken stock and cornstarch together; make a well in the middle of the vegetables and add cornstarch mixture. Mix well and make sure it doesn't burn. Stir in the soy sauce and garnish with roasted pine nuts. Serve with your favorite rice dish.

SPINACH CHEESECAKE

a savory main course or appetizer

serves 8

6 tbsp.	butter	90 mL
1 cup	fine Ritz cracker crumbs	250 mL
¼ cup	grated Parmesan cheese	50 mL
2 bunches	spinach, cleaned, chopped	2 bunches
2 tbsp.	butter or margarine	30 mL
2	medium-sized onions, diced	2
8 ozs.	cream cheese	250 mL
11 ozs.	sour cream (1½ cups plus 2 tsp.)	385 mL
4	eggs, lightly beaten	4
4½ oz.	grated feta cheese	135 mL

Melt butter; add crumbs; add Parmesan cheese. Spread crumb mixture and press evenly in 10" (25 cm) springform pan, pushing crust three-quarters of the way up the side of the pan so the cheesecake will have a crust around the sides as well as the bottom. Blanch spinach; set aside to drain.

In a medium-sized frying pan, melt butter; sauté onion; add spinach and set aside. Cool to room temperature. Combine cream cheese and sour cream; add eggs. Add spinach and onion, blending until smooth. Pour on top of crumb mixture and bake in 350°F (180°C) oven for 1¼ hours, until golden brown. Top with grated feta cheese. Slice into wedges and serve with sliced fresh fruit. Serve hot.

See photograph page 33.

MUSHROOM & NUT TERRINE

serves 8

3 tbsp.	butter	45 mL
2 lbs.	mushrooms	1 kg
2	garlic cloves, minced	2
2 tbsp.	port or sherry	30 mL
3	eggs	3
½ cup	cream	125 mL
1 cup	grated sharp Cheddar cheese	250 mL
½ cup	grated Gouda cheese	125 mL
¾ cup	almonds or pecans, blanched	175 mL

Heat butter in a large sauté pan; add mushrooms; sauté at high heat until browned. Add garlic and port and cook another minute; drain and cool. Combine eggs, cream and cheeses in another bowl; add mushroom mixture and nuts. Line a 3½" x 11¼" x 3" (9 cm x 29 cm x 8 cm) loaf pan with greased wax paper; pour in mushroom mixture and bake in 325°F (160°C) oven for 1½ hours, in a water bath*. Remove terrine from the oven and cool overnight in the refrigerator. Slice and serve with Kumquat and Brandy Sauce, page 27, and melba toast or toasted English muffins.

* water bath — means: place loaf pan in a larger baking pan, pour 1" (2.5 cm) of hot water around the outside of the loaf pan.

HERB SOUFFLÉ

serves 6

4½ tbsp.	butter	67 mL
1½ tbsp.	all-purpose flour	22 mL
1 cup	milk	250 mL
3	eggs, separated	3
1 tbsp.	chopped fresh parsley	15 mL
½ cup	chopped fresh basil	125 mL
1 tbsp.	chopped fresh dill	15 mL
1 tbsp.	chopped green onion	15 mL

Grease 6, ½-cup (125 mL) soufflé dishes. Melt butter in saucepan; stir in flour and continue stirring for 1 minute. Remove from heat; gradually add milk. Return to heat until thickened. Put in mixing bowl; cover and cool. Add egg yolks and spices. Beat egg whites in a separate bowl, until soft peaks are formed. Fold into yolk mixture and pour into greased soufflé cups. Bake in 350°F (180°C) oven for 15 minutes. Serve with Pimiento Sauce, recipe follows.

pimiento sauce

14 oz.	canned or bottled pimientos, drained	398 mL
½ cup	whipping cream	125 mL
2 tsp.	sugar	10 mL
1¼ tbsp.	brandy or cognac	19 mL

Drain pimientos. Combine all ingredients in a blender or food processor and blend until smooth. Pour into saucepan and heat until thickened. Serve on Herb Soufflé with roasted peppers.

CRÊPES

MEDITERRANEAN CRÊPES

with tomato herb filling

serves 6

basic crêpe batter - makes 12-16 crêpes

1 cup	all-purpose flour	250 mL
4	eggs	4
4 tbsp.	vegetable oil	60 mL
1½ cups	milk	375 mL

Combine all ingredients and blend until smooth. Let stand at least 1 hour. Use 6" (15 cm) teflon pan to make crêpes. Stack crêpes, using wax paper between each crêpe. Set aside to cool. Prepare filling below.

tomato herb filling

3 tbsp.	olive oil	45 mL
1	onion, finely diced	1
1	medium green pepper, diced	1
4	medium zucchini, quartered, diced	4
3	garlic cloves, minced	3
4	tomatoes, finely diced	4
2 tsp.	tomato paste	10 mL
¼ tsp.	oregano	1 mL
¼ tsp.	basil	1 mL
½ tsp.	sugar	2 mL
1 tbsp.	white or red wine	15 mL
1 tbsp.	chopped parsley	15 mL
2 tbsp.	grated feta cheese	30 mL

In a large sauté pan, heat oil; sauté onions, peppers, zucchini and garlic; cook until al dente. Add remaining ingredients, except feta cheese, and sauté until tender. Fold crêpes in quarters; assemble 4 per plate. Put vegetable mixture in middle of crêpes and top with grated feta cheese. Serve at once.

wine selection

Orvieto

TRIO CRÊPE BAKE

serves 4

16	crêpes	16
1 cup	minced cooked spinach	250 mL
¼ cup	chopped, hard-boiled egg	50 mL
1 cup	minced cooked carrots	250 mL
⅛ cup	shredded coconut	25 mL
1 cup	minced cooked squash	250 mL
¼ cup	raisins	50 mL
½ cup	finely chopped chives or green onions	125 mL
½ cup	ricotta cheese	125 mL
½ cup	grated Cheddar cheese	125 mL
½ cup	grated Gouda cheese	125 mL
½ cup	fine bread crumbs	125 mL
2	eggs	2
¼ cup	brandy	50 mL
	salt and pepper to taste	

Prepare crêpes, see recipe, page 80. Lay 1 crêpe on baking dish; spread with ⅛ of the spinach and top with ¼ of the cooked egg. Lay second crêpe on top and spread with ¼ of the carrot and sprinkle with ¼ of the shredded coconut. Lay third crêpe on top and spread with ¼ of the squash and top with ¼ of the raisins. Lay fourth crêpe on top and spread with ⅛ of the spinach. Combine the remaining ingredients and spread over spinach. Repeat layers until all crêpes and fillings have been used. Bake in 400°F (200°C) oven for 10-15 minutes. Cut into 4 wedges to serve.

serving suggestions

Serve with salad of your choice. Place on plates and decorate with fresh fruit and edible flowers.

wine selection

Côtes du Rhône

S E N S A T I O N A L   P E A S

serves 4

16	crêpes	16
3 tbsp.	butter	45 mL
⅛ cup	finely diced chives	25 mL
1 cup	sliced mushrooms	250 mL
1½ cups	peas	375 mL
½ cup	pearl onions	125 mL
¼ cup	brandy	50 mL
1 cup	whole cream (divided)	250 mL
8 oz.	cream cheese	250 g
1½ cups	grated Edam cheese	375 mL

Prepare crêpes, see recipe, page 80. Melt butter; add chives and mushrooms; sauté for 10 minutes. Drain off liquid. Add peas, pearl onions and sauté for 2 minutes. Add brandy and ¼ cup (50 mL) cream; continue cooking by bringing to a boil; reduce the contents to ⅓. Once the liquid has been reduced, add cream cheese and melt. Arrange crêpes, folded into quarters, in baking dish; pour vegetable mixture over crêpes; top with remaining cream; sprinkle with grated Edam cheese. Bake in 400°F (200°C) oven for 15-20 minutes.

P O T A T O   C R E A M   C R Ê P E S

serves 4

16	crêpes	16
1 cup	mashed potatoes	250 mL
¼ cup	finely diced chives	50 mL
2 tbsp.	dillweed	30 mL
1 cup	cottage cheese or ricotta cheese	250 mL
2 cups	whole cream	500 mL
1 cup	grated medium Cheddar cheese	250 mL

POTATO CREAM CRÊPES

(continued)

Prepare crêpes, see recipe page 80. Mix together potatoes, chives, dillweed and cottage or ricotta cheese. Roll potato filling into crêpes; place crêpes side by side in baking dish. Pour cream over crêpes, until it is ⅓ of the way up the crêpes. Top with grated Cheddar cheese. Bake in a 375°F (190°C) oven for 15-20 minutes. Serve with a salad of your choice.

wine selection

German Niersteiner

CARROT CHEESE CRÊPES

serves 6

12	crêpes	12
1 cup	shredded carrot	250 mL
6 oz.	cream cheese	170 g
2	eggs	2
2 tbsp.	dillweed	30 mL
½ cup	shredded acorn squash	125 mL
1 cup	whole cream	250 mL
1 cup	mozzarella cheese	250 mL

Prepare crêpes, see recipe page 80. Combine carrots, cream cheese, eggs, dillweed and squash until blended. Roll carrot filling in crêpes; place in baking pan (2 per serving). Pour cream ¼ way up the crêpes. Top with grated mozzarella cheese. Bake in 400°F (200°C) oven until browned, about 15-20 minutes.

wine selection

Light Chianti

MUSHROOM CRÊPES

serves 6

12	crêpes	12
2 tbsp.	olive oil	30 mL
3	garlic cloves, minced	3
4	green onions, diced	4
1 lb.	mushrooms, sliced	500 g
8 oz.	cream cheese	250 g
	salt and pepper to taste	
½ cup	grated Gouda cheese	125 mL

Prepare crêpes, see recipe page 80. Heat olive oil; add minced garlic and green onion. Sauté for 30 seconds; add mushrooms and sauté until tender. Save a few mushrooms for garnish. Remove mushrooms from heat and mix in cream cheese. Add salt and pepper to taste. Fill center of crêpe with mushroom mixture and roll. Place seam side down in baking dish. Top with reserved sautéed mushrooms and Gouda cheese. Bake at 400°F (200°C) oven for 10-15 minutes.

serving suggestions

Serve with a Caesar salad. Decorate the crêpes with a couple of garden pansies (peach, orange and yellow), or garnish with chopped chives or parsley.

wine selection

Gewurztraminer

C R E O L E   C R Ê P E S

32	crêpes	32
2 tbsp.	butter	30 mL
2	large onions, medium diced	2
4	green peppers, medium diced	4
½	celery stalk, diced	½
½ lb.	mushrooms, sliced	250 g
7 cups	crushed tomatoes	1.75 L
4 tbsp.	tomato paste	60 mL
1	bay leaf	1
2 tbsp.	oregano	30 mL
2 tbsp.	sweet basil	30 mL
1 tbsp.	sugar	15 mL
2 tbsp.	minced garlic	30 mL
dash	Tabasco sauce	dash
	salt and pepper to taste	
	parsley for garnish	
	grated Cheddar cheese for garnish	

Prepare crêpes, see recipe page 80. Melt butter; sauté vegetables in order given, with 3 minute intervals, until all vegetables are cooked al dente. Add tomatoes and seasonings; bring to a boil; reduce heat and simmer until the sauce reduces to the desired thickness. Place 4 crêpes, folded into quarters, on each plate making a circle. Top with Creole sauce. Garnish with parsley and grated Cheddar cheese.

wine selection

A full-bodied Chianti

SPINACH CRÊPES

6	crêpes	6
2 tbsp.	butter	30 mL
1	small onion, finely chopped	1
2 bunches	spinach, cleaned	2 bunches
1 cup	ricotta cheese	250 mL
1	small garlic clove, minced	1
1 tbsp.	lemon pepper	15 mL
½ cup	fine bread crumbs	125 mL
1	egg	1
2	hard-boiled eggs, peeled, sliced, for garnish	2

Prepare crêpes, see recipe page 80. Melt butter and sauté onion until transparent. Add spinach, cover and steam until spinach changes color. Drain off liquid; place spinach mixture and remaining ingredients, except for hard-boiled egg, in food processor. Blend ingredients just until they hold together. Do NOT liquify. Place a crêpe in a quiche pan, top with ¼ cup (50 mL) of spinach mixture. Repeat until you reach a height of 2½ inches (6 cm), then spread remaining spinach mixture over the crêpes. Bake in a 400°F (200°C) oven for 15 minutes. Slice stacked crêpe into 4 wedges; garnish with hard-boiled egg. Serve with a tossed salad.

wine selection

Rioja from Spain - of course!

MEXICAN CORN CRÊPES

serves 4

16	crêpes	16
2 tbsp.	butter	30 mL
¼ cup	finely diced chives	50 mL
1	green pepper, seeded, finely sliced	1
2 cups	corn niblets, drained	500 mL
4 oz.	jar pimientoes, drained, finely diced	125 g
1¼ cups	refried beans	300 mL
1 cup	grated medium Cheddar cheese	250 mL
	garnish with sliced black olives, diced tomatoes, green onions, jalapeño peppers, sour cream, salsa	

MEXICAN CORN CRÊPES

Prepare crêpes, see recipe page 80. Melt butter; add chives and green peppers; sauté 5-10 minutes. Add corn and pimientoes; sauté for 5 more minutes. Stir in refried beans. Remove from heat. Roll corn filling into crêpes, place in a baking dish, seam side down, and top with grated Cheddar cheese. Bake in 400°F (200°C) oven for 10-15 minutes. After crêpes are baked, garnish with olives, tomatoes, green onions, jalapeño peppers, sour cream, and salsa. Put the sour cream and salsa in separate bowls. Serve with tossed salad, cornbread and honey.

wine selection

Mexican beer!!

BROC AND CAULI CRÊPES

serves 4

16	crêpes	16
2 tbsp.	butter	30 mL
2	garlic cloves, minced	2
1½ cups	small broccoli florets	375 mL
1½ cups	small cauliflower florets	375 mL
½ cup	pearl onions	125 mL
⅓ cup	whipping cream	75 mL
12 oz.	cream cheese	340 g
	salt and pepper to taste	
2 tbsp.	cornstarch	30 mL
2 tbsp.	cold water	30 mL
¼ cup	brandy	50 mL
2 cups	grated sharp Cheddar cheese	500 mL

Prepare crêpes, see recipe page 80. Melt butter; add garlic, vegetables and cream; bring to a boil. When vegetables are soft, yet crunchy, blend in cream cheese and seasonings. Remove from heat. This mixture should be thick; if too runny, add combined cornstarch and water; cook until thickened. Roll vegetable mixture into crêpes. Place in buttered baking dish; pour brandy over and top with grated sharp Cheddar cheese. Bake in 400°F (200°C) oven for 15-20 minutes. Serve at once.

wine selection

Alsace Pinot Blanc

APPLE AND CARROT CRÊPES

serves 4

16	crêpes	16
3 tbsp.	butter	45 mL
¼	onion, minced	¼
¼ cup	grated carrot	50 mL
¼ cup	peeled, diced apple (Granny Smith preferred)	50 mL
1	bay leaf	1
⅛ cup	Calvados*	25 mL
½ cup	whole cream	125 mL
½ cup	grated Cheddar cheese	125 mL
2	eggs	2
½ cup	bread crumbs	125 g
	salt and pepper to taste	
	spiced apple rings for garnish	

Prepare crêpes, see recipe page 80. Melt butter in sauté pan; add onion and sauté for 5 minutes. Add carrots and apple; sauté an additional 5 minutes. Remove from heat and place mixture into a bowl. Return pan to heat and add bay leaf, Calvados and cream; bring to a boil and reduce by ⅓. Remove from heat. Add remaining ingredients, except for spiced apple rings, to apple mixture; mix thoroughly and roll into crêpe shells. Place crêpes, seam side down, in baking dish and pour cream mixture over top; bake in 400°F (200°C) oven for 10-15 minutes. Serve hot with spiced apple rings.

* A French, apple-based brandy, very light, yet fruitful in flavor — substitute brandy if you wish.

wine selection

Riesling from B.C.

PASTAS

B A S I C P A S T A

yields 1 lb. (500 g); serves 4

2 cups	all-purpose flour	500 g
5	eggs	5
1 tsp.	salt	5 mL

Combine all ingredients into a ball, reserving ¼ cup (50 mL) flour for dusting. After forming ball, slice into 6 equal parts. Roll out dough in pasta machine, then use pasta machine to cut into desired thickness and width (as for fettucini or linguini). Cook pasta for 6-8 minutes in boiling salted and oiled water. Drain and serve with your favorite toppings or sauce.

B L A C K P A S T A

satiny sheen and texture

yields 1 lb. (500 g); serves 4

2 cups	all-purpose flour	500 g
⅛ cup	squid ink	25 mL
3	large eggs	3
1 tsp.	salt	15 mL
¼ cup	all-purpose flour (to dust pasta)	50 mL

Combine all ingredients into a ball, reserving ¼ cup (50 mL) flour for dusting. After forming ball, slice into 6 equal parts. Roll out dough in pasta machine; then use pasta machine to cut into desired thickness and width (as for fettucini or linguini). This pasta makes a beautiful presentation foil for fresh seafood or vegetables in a light sauce.

note

Remember to use hand crank machine if moist pasta dough is used, otherwise it will tear very easily. Keep the pasta dusted with flour to prevent sticking and/or ripping.

BLACK PEPPER PASTA

yields 1 lb. (500 g); serves 4

2 cups	all-purpose flour	500 g
5	eggs	5
¼ cup	peppercorns, crushed*	50 mL
1 tsp.	salt	5 mL

Combine all ingredients into a ball, reserving ¼ cup (50 mL) flour for dusting. After forming ball, slice into 6 equal parts. Roll out dough in pasta machine; then use pasta machine to cut into desired thickness and width (as for fettucini or linguini).

*measure out ¼ cup (50 mL) of peppercorns, then crush them.

WHOLE-WHEAT PASTA

yields 1 lb. (500 g); serves 4

1 cup	whole-wheat flour	250 g
1 cup	all-purpose flour	250 g
5	eggs	5
1 tsp.	salt	5 mL

Combine all ingredients into a ball, reserving ¼ cup (50 mL) flour for dusting. After forming ball, slice into 6 equal parts. Roll out dough in pasta machine; then use pasta machine to cut into desired thickness and width (as in fettucini or linguini) .

note

Remember to use hand crank machine if moist pasta dough is used, otherwise it will tear very easily. Keep the pasta dusted with flour to prevent sticking and/or ripping.

S P I N A C H   P A S T A

yields 1 lb. (500 g); serves 4

¼ cup	spinach purée	50 mL
2 cups	all-purpose flour	500 g
3	large eggs	3
1 tsp.	salt	5 mL

Combine all ingredients into a ball, reserving ¼ cup (50 mL) flour for dusting. After forming ball, slice into 6 equal parts. Roll out dough in pasta machine; then use pasta machine to cut into desired thickness and width (as for fettucini or linguini).

S W E E T   B A S I L   P A S T A

yields 1 lb. (500 g); serves 4

2 cups	flour	500 g
5	eggs	5
1 tsp.	salt	5 mL
2 tbsp.	sweet basil	30 g

Combine all ingredients into a ball, reserving ¼ cup (50 mL) flour for dusting. After forming ball, slice into 6 equal parts. Roll out dough in pasta machine; then use pasta machine to cut into desired thickness and width (as for fettucini or linguini).

note

Remember to use hand crank machine if moist pasta dough is used, otherwise it will tear very easily. Keep the pasta dusted with flour to prevent sticking and/or ripping.

T O M A T O   P A S T A

or tomato herb* pasta

yields 1 lb. (500 g); serves 4

2 cups	all-purpose flour	500 g
3	large eggs	3
1 tsp.	salt	5 mL
¼ cup	tomato purée or tomato paste	50 mL
1-2 tbsp.	chopped mixed herbs * (optional)	15-30 mL

Combine all ingredients into a ball, reserving ¼ cup (50 mL) flour for dusting. After forming ball, slice into 6 equal parts. Roll out dough in pasta machine; then use pasta machine to cut into desired thickness and width (as for fettucini or linguini).

*Try basil, oregano, parsley, etc.

W H O L E - W H E A T   F E T T U C I N I

with pine nuts

serves 6

1½ recipes	Whole-Wheat Pasta, page 91	1½ recipes
2 tbsp.	butter	30 mL
3	green onions, chopped	3
¼ cup	pine nuts	50 mL
2 tbsp.	chopped parsley, squeezed dry	30 mL
1 tbsp.	sweet basil	15 mL
	salt and pepper to taste	
¼ cup	ricotta cheese	50 mL
¼ cup	whipping cream	50 mL

Prepare pasta and cut into fettucini noodles. Boil for 6-8 minutes and set aside to drain. Melt butter; add green onions and pine nuts; sauté for 3 minutes. Add parsley, basil, salt, pepper, ricotta cheese and cream. Heat until smooth. Toss lightly with noodles. Serve at once.

wine selection

Bardolino

TOMATO & SPINACH PASTA

serves 4

½ recipe	Tomato Pasta, page 93	½ recipe
½ recipe	Spinach Pasta, page 92	½ recipe
2 tbsp.	butter	30 mL
¼ cup	finely diced chives	50 mL
¼ cup	whipping cream	50 mL
	salt and pepper to taste	
¼ cup	each, grated Gorgonzola, Parmesan, Fontina cheeses	50 mL
	fresh basil for garnish	

Make ½ recipe each of Tomato and Spinach Pastas. Cook, drain and set aside. Melt butter; add chives and sauté for 30 seconds. Add cream, salt and pepper. Bring to a boil; add cheeses. Toss pastas with cheese mixture. Garnish with a sprig of fresh basil.

wine selection

Zinfandel

JULIENNE OF VEGETABLES

serves 4

1 lb.	your favorite pasta	500 g
3 tbsp.	butter	45 mL
3	garlic cloves, minced	3
⅛ cup	finely chopped shallots	25 mL
¼ cup	each, julienned turnips, carrots, celery	50 mL
½ cup	julienned green peppers	125 mL
½ cup	sliced mushrooms	125 mL
	salt and pepper to taste	
2 tbsp.	sweet basil	30 mL
1 cup	puréed tomatoes	250 mL
¼ cup	whole cream	50 mL
	grated Parmesan cheese for garnish	

JULIENNE OF VEGETABLES

(continued)

Prepare pasta, drain and set aside. Melt butter, add garlic and shallots. Add and sauté vegetables in order given, in 5-minute intervals. Once all vegetables have been added, add spices and puréed tomatoes. Bring to a boil for 10 minutes. Add pasta and cream and toss. Serve hot. Top with grated Parmesan cheese.

wine selection

California Sauvignon Blanc

FETTUCINI ANTONIO

serves 6

1 recipe	fettucini, page 90	1 recipe
3 tbsp.	butter	45 mL
1	small onion, finely diced	1
1	garlic clove, minced	1
1 cup	broccoli florets	250 mL
	salt and pepper to taste	
¼ cup	whipping cream	50 mL
½ cup	grated Parmesan cheese	125 mL
	chopped parsley for garnish	

Cut pasta dough into fettucini noodles. Cook 6-8 minutes in boiling, salted and oiled water. Drain and set aside. Melt butter; add onion and garlic; add broccoli florets and salt and pepper to taste. Add noodles and toss until mixed thoroughly. Add cream and boil tossing lightly, until cream thickens. Add Parmesan cheese. Place on plates and serve at once. Garnish with chopped parsley.

wine selection

Full-bodied Red Wine

TOMATO & ARTICHOKES

with pasta

serves 4-6

1 lb.	pasta	500 g
¼ cup	olive oil	50 mL
¼ cup	lemon juice	50 mL
4	tomatoes, chopped	4
½ cup	black olives, seeded	125 mL
1 cup	drained and chopped artichoke hearts	250 mL
1 tbsp.	chopped fresh basil	15 mL
2 tbsp.	chopped fresh parsley	30 mL

Using pasta of your choice, cook, drain and set aside. In a saucepan, sauté all remaining ingredients until hot. Add pasta and toss until all is heated through. Serve at once.

note

Artichoke hearts are canned or bottled. If using fresh artichokes, use only hearts and blanch them first for about 2-3 minutes.

wine selection

California Chardonnay

PASTA PRIMAVERA

serves 4

1 recipe	Black Pepper Pasta, page 91, or Sweet Basil Pasta, page 92	1 recipe
2 tbsp.	butter	30 mL
⅛ cup	finely diced onion	25 mL
2	garlic cloves, minced	2
½	red pepper, finely sliced	½
½	yellow pepper, finely sliced	½
¼ cup	broccoli florets	50 mL
¼ cup	cauliflower florets	50 mL
1 cup	whipping cream	250 mL
20	snowpeas, cleaned, tipped (5 per plate)	20
¼ cup	Parmesan cheese	50 mL

PASTA PRIMAVERA

(continued)

Prepare pasta, drain and set aside. Melt butter; add onion and garlic and sauté for 1 minute. Add peppers, broccoli and cauliflower and sauté for 10 minutes. Add cream and bring to a boil for 4 minutes. Add snow peas and Parmesan cheese. Add pasta and toss. Serve at once with fresh bread or buns.

See photograph page 69.

wine selection

A Red Bordeaux

TRI-COLOR FETTUCINI

serves 4

⅓ recipe	each, of 3 pasta recipes	⅓ recipe
3 tbsp.	butter	45 mL
2	garlic cloves, minced	2
½ cup	diced green onion	125 mL
½ cup	sliced pepper (your choice of color)	125 mL
1 cup	snow peas, cleaned	250 mL
1 cup	whipping cream	250 mL
1 tsp.	ground nutmeg	5 mL
	salt and pepper to taste	
¼ cup	grated Parmesan cheese	50 mL

Boil pasta; drain and set aside. Melt butter; add garlic, onion and pepper and sauté for 5 minutes. Add snow peas, cream and nutmeg; bring to a boil for 6 minutes. Add pasta and toss lightly. Add salt, pepper and cheese. Serve hot.

wine selection

A Fresh Young Chenin Blanc

BLACK PASTA SUPREME

serves 4

1 recipe	Black Pasta, page 90	1 recipe
20	cucumber balls	20
20	carrot balls	20
20	acorn squash balls	20
3 tbsp.	butter	45 mL
2	garlic cloves, minced	2
½ tsp.	grated ginger root	2 mL
½ cup	finely chopped onion	125 mL
½	red pepper, finely sliced	½
1 cup	sliced mushrooms	250 g
1 cup	whipping cream	250 mL
¼ cup	brandy or Grand Marnier	50 mL
	salt and pepper to taste	
	grated feta cheese for garnish	

Boil pasta, drain and set aside. Using a melon baller, make cucumber, carrot and squash balls. Melt butter and add garlic, ginger and onions. Sauté for 5 minutes. Add pepper, mushrooms and all vegetable balls. Add cream and bring to a boil until tender. Add brandy and spices. Add pasta and toss lightly. Serve hot and garnish with grated feta cheese.

note

This melon baller is the size of a pea. It can be bought at kitchen specialty stores.

DESSERTS

M E L O N   I C E

serves 6

2 cups	melon purée, 14 oz. (400 g) of melon meat	500 mL
½ cup	sugar	125 mL
1 cup	water	250 mL
2	egg whites	2
	melon slices for garnish	
	mint leaves for garnish	

Prepare melon purée; try your favorites, watermelon, cantaloupe, honeydew, winter melon, ogen melon, muskmelon, etc. Combine sugar and water in a saucepan. Constantly stir over medium heat without boiling. Simmer, uncovered, for 10 minutes. Remove and cool to room temperature. Stir in melon purée; pour mixture into a nonstick pan; cover and freeze until partially set. Process or blend egg whites and melon mixture until smooth. Freeze overnight. When serving, garnish with a slice of melon and a mint leaf.

variations

Try other Fruit Ice flavors using papaya, mango, peach, raspberry, etc.

F I G S   &   C R E A M

serves 4

1 cup	cream	250 mL
½ cup	sugar	125 mL
¼ cup	lemon juice	50 mL
1 cup	raisins	250 mL
¼ cup	shredded or flaked coconut	50 mL
8	figs, quartered	8
1½ cups	Champagne	375 mL

Combine cream, sugar, lemon juice, raisins and coconut; bring to a boil; add figs; bring to a boil again. Reduce heat; simmer for 5-10 minutes until figs are tender; Cool. Serve by placing figs in a bowl; top with raisin and coconut sauce and sprinkle with Champagne. Serve with Champagne.

P E A R D E L I G H T

serves 6

6	pears, peeled, cored	6
1 cup	butter	250 mL
1 tbsp.	maple syrup	15 mL
½ cup	chopped pecans	125 mL
½ cup	shredded coconut	125 mL

Prepare pears. In a sauté pan, combine butter, maple syrup, pecans and coconut. Stuff pears with nut, coconut mixture; stand them up in a large baking dish and drizzle remaining sauce over them. Bake pears at 400°F (200°C) until done, about 20 minutes. Top with your favorite fruit purée or chocolate sauce and a mint leaf.

B A N A N A S U P R E M E

serves 6

6	large bananas, peeled, cut into thirds	6
6 tbsp.	brown sugar	90 mL
1 cup	grated milk chocolate	250 mL
¼ cup	white rum	50 mL
	vanilla ice cream	
	whipped cream for garnish	
	cherries or fresh berries for garnish	

Grease an 8" x 8" (20 cm x 20 cm) pan; place bananas in pan; sprinkle with brown sugar and chocolate; pour white rum over entire mixture. Bake in 400°F (200°C) oven until bananas are soft. Arrange 3 banana thirds over each serving of vanilla ice cream; top with sauce mixture. Top with whipped cream and a cherry.

CHOCOLATE MOUSSE

with raspberry & papaya coulis

serves 6-8

12 oz.	milk chocolate or Belgian dark chocolate	340 g
1 cup	whipping cream	250 mL
2 tbsp.	Cognac	30 mL
4	egg whites	4
½ cup	berry sugar	125 mL
⅔ cup	whipping cream, whipped	150 mL
	chocolate curls for garnish	
	toasted almonds for garnish	
	Raspberry Coulis, below	
	Papaya Coulis, below	

Melt chocolate. Combine melted chocolate, whipping cream and cognac in a food processor and blend until smooth. Beat egg whites while gradually adding sugar, until they form soft peaks. Fold into chocolate mixture. Pour into individual serving dishes or a serving bowl and refrigerate until needed. Serve with a dollop of whipped cream. Top with chocolate curls and toasted almonds. Serve with Raspberry Coulis and/or Papaya Coulis, or garnish with fresh raspberries.

raspberry coulis

1½ cups	raspberries	375 mL
¼ cup	icing sugar	50 mL

Blend well in food processor. Place in refrigerator until needed. Makes 1 cup (250 mL).

papaya coulis

2 cups	papaya meat	500 mL
½ cup	icing sugar	125 mL

Blend well in food processor. Place in refrigerator until needed. Makes 1½ cups (375 mL).

See photograph on opposite page.

Chocolate Mousse, page 102
with Raspberry Coulis and Payaya Coulis, page 102

C A R R O T   C O O K I E S

makes 2 dozen

¾ cup	butter	175 mL
1 cup	sugar	250 mL
1	large egg	1
1½ cups	mashed cooked carrots	375 mL
½ cup	currants	125 mL
2¼ cups	flour	550 mL
2½ tsp.	baking powder	12 mL
1 tsp.	vanilla	5 mL
½ tsp.	allspice	2 mL

Cream butter and sugar together; add egg, cooked carrot and currants. Fold in flour, baking powder, vanilla and allspice. Drop on greased cookie sheet by tablespoonful (15 mL) and bake in 400°F (200°C) oven for 10-12 minutes.

Z U C C H I N I   F L O W E R   C O O K I E S

an italian specialty

makes 12

1	large egg	1
1 cup	cold water	250 mL
1¼ cups	flour	300 mL
12	zucchini flowers, ripe	12
	vegetable oil for deep-frying	
	icing sugar	

Prepare batter by combining egg, cold water and flour. Blend until smooth. Refrigerate overnight. Wash flowers; towel dry. Heat oil to 365°F (185°C). Dip each blossom in batter and deep-fry in hot oil until golden brown. Drain on paper towel; dust with icing sugar.

S Q U A S H   D O U G H N U T S

makes 24

1½ cups	sugar	375 mL
1 tbsp.	butter	15 mL
2	eggs	2
¾ cup	mashed cooked acorn squash	175 mL
1 tsp.	vanilla	5 mL
1½ tsp.	baking soda	7 mL
2 tsp.	baking powder	10 mL
½ tsp.	salt	2 mL
½ tsp.	nutmeg	2 mL
½ tsp.	ginger	2 mL
1 cup	buttermilk	250 mL
3¼ cups	flour	800 mL

Beat together sugar, butter, eggs, squash, vanilla, baking soda, baking powder and spices; fold in buttermilk and flour. Roll out dough; cut out doughnuts ¾" (2 cm) thick. Heat oil to 365°F (185°C); deep-fry doughnuts, a few at a time, on both sides until brown, about 3 minutes, each side. Roll in sugar and serve.

S W E E T   P O T A T O   P I E

serves 6-8

1	9" (23 cm) pie crust, unbaked	1
2 cups	mashed cooked sweet potatoes	500 mL
3	large eggs	3
¼ cup	whipping cream	50 mL
¾ cup	white sugar	175 mL
1 cup	crushed walnuts or pecans	250 mL
2 tbsp.	cinnamon	30 mL
½ tsp.	allspice	2 mL

SWEET POTATO PIE

(continued)

Prepare pie crust. Combine remaining ingredients in blender or food processor and blend until smooth. Pour into pie shell; bake in 350°F (180°C) oven until firm, about 50 minutes.

note

You can check to see if the pie is ready by placing a toothpick in the center of the pie and pulling it out to see if it comes out clean. If it does come out clean, it's ready.

BROWNIE PIZZA

the vegetable version

serves 14

¾ cup	corn syrup	175 mL
⅓ cup	whipping cream	75 mL
8 oz.	semisweet chocolate	250 g
½ cup	butter or margarine	125 mL
½ cup	sugar	125 mL
2	eggs	2
½ tsp.	vanilla	2 mL
¾ cup	flour	175 mL
½ tsp.	salt	2 mL
¼ cup	diced celery	50 mL
¼ cup	diced carrots	50 mL
¼ cup	diced leeks	50 mL

Grease and flour 12" (30 cm) pizza pan. In a saucepan, bring syrup and cream to a boil over medium heat, stirring occasionally. Add chocolate and stir until melted; add butter and sugar; stir until melted. Remove from heat. Stir in eggs and vanilla gradually. Add flour, salt and vegetables. Pour into pan and bake at 350°F (180°C) for 20 minutes. Cool and serve with sorbet or ice cream.

BANANA-ZUCCHINI CAKE

with chocolate macadamia nut frosting

serves 12

3 cups	all-purpose flour	750 mL
3½ cups	sugar	875 mL
1 tbsp.	salt	15 mL
3 tbsp.	baking powder	45 mL
1 tbsp.	baking soda	15 mL
1 cup	lard or shortening	250 mL
1½ cups	puréed ripe bananas	375 mL
1 cup	puréed zucchini	250 mL
8	eggs	8
1 cup	milk	250 mL
	vanilla to taste	

Mix first 8 items for 5-7 minutes; add eggs and milk, alternating in 3 parts, scraping down the bowl each time. Line a 9" x 3" x 2" (22 cm x 33 cm x 5 cm) pan or 2 loaf pans with greased wax paper. Bake at 350°F (180°C) for approximately 1 hour, or until done. Cool and frost with Chocolate Macadamia Nut Frosting.

chocolate macadamia nut frosting

½ cup	butter or margarine	125 mL
2 tbsp.	cocoa powder	30 mL
1 tbsp.	cream or milk	15 mL
2 cups	icing sugar	500 mL
½ cup	macadamia nut purée	125 mL

Whip butter; add cocoa and cream. Slowly add icing sugar and beat until smooth; add nut purée. Spread on cooled cake.

C A R R O T   S P I C E   C A K E

with orange-lemon cream cheese frosting

serves 10-12

1 cup	all-purpose flour	250 mL
1 tsp.	baking soda	5 mL
½ tsp.	cinnamon	2 mL
½ tsp.	cloves	2 mL
2 tsp.	allspice	10 mL
1 cup	brown sugar (packed)	250 mL
½ cup	grated carrots	375 mL
½ cup	sultanas	125 mL
½ cup	chopped walnuts	125 mL
⅔ cup	oil	150 mL
2	eggs, lightly beaten	2

Sift flour, soda and spices into bowl; stir in sugar, carrots, sultanas and nuts; stir in combined oil and eggs. Beat on medium speed with electric mixer for 5 minutes. Pour into greased 5" x 9" (12 cm x 23 cm) loaf pan and bake at 350°F (180°C) for 1 hour. Cool 5 minutes in pan, and turn out on wire rack. When cool, frost with Orange-Lemon Cream Cheese Frosting.

orange-lemon cream cheese frosting

4 oz.	cream cheese	125 g
¼ cup	soft butter	50 mL
1 tsp.	grated lemon rind	5 mL
1 tsp.	grated orange rind	25 mL
1 oz.	lemon juice	25 mL
1 oz.	orange juice	25 mL
2 cups	icing sugar	500 mL

Combine all ingredients and beat on medium speed with electric mixer until smooth. Spread over loaf; slice and serve.

wine selection

A Sauternes - from France, of course!

P U M P K I N   C H E E S E C A K E

a velvety texture

serves 12

1 cup	ground vanilla wafers	250 g
¼ cup	white sugar	50 mL
¼ cup	melted butter or margarine	50 mL
2½ lbs.	cream cheese	1.25 kg
⅓ cup	white sugar	75 mL
1½ cups	brown sugar	375 mL
1 cup	puréed pumpkin meat	250 mL
2 tsp.	ground cinnamon	10 mL
1 tsp.	ground allspice	5 mL
¼ cup	Baileys Irish Cream	50 mL
3	large eggs	3
2	large egg yolks	2

Combine all crust ingredients and line bottom of 10" (3 L) springform pan. Set aside while you prepare filling.

Beat cream cheese until smooth, about 10-15 minutes. Continue to beat and gradually add both white and brown sugar until blended. Beat in puréed pumpkin meat until smooth. Add spices and Baileys Irish cream. Scrape down sides, and beat until smooth. Beat in eggs and egg yolks. Pour batter into springform pan and bake in the oven at 350°F (180°C) for 1½ hours. Turn oven off and open oven door part way, leaving cheesecake in the oven to cool to room temperature (about 2-3 hours). Place cheesecake in the refrigerator and leave overnight or at least 6 hours. Slice and serve with whipped cream and shaved chocolate.

variations

Try gingersnap crumbs or chocolate wafers instead of vanilla wafers for the crust. Try Grand Marnier liqueur or Apricot Brandy instead of Baileys Irish Cream. Garnish with minced crystallized ginger if using gingersnaps in the crust.

wine selection

A cream sherry

STEAMED CARROT PUDDING

serves 6-8

½ cup	shredded apple	125 mL
1 cup	shredded potato	250 mL
1 cup	shredded carrot	250 mL
1 cup	brown sugar	250 mL
½ cup	flour	125 mL
1 tsp.	baking soda	5 mL
1 tsp.	salt	5 mL
1 tsp.	cinnamon	5 mL
¼ tsp.	nutmeg	1 mL
½ tsp.	allspice	2 mL
1 cup	bread crumbs	250 mL
1 cup	raisins	250 mL
1 cup	currants	250 mL

Combine apple, potato, carrots and brown sugar. Combine all remaining ingredients and add to apple mixture. Mix and put into 6-cup (1.5 L) greased mold. Cover with foil and tie securely. Put in water bath* and steam for 3-3½ hours.

*Water bath means to place baking dish in a pan filled with ½" (1.3 cm) of water. This will keep the product you are cooking moist throughout the cooking process.

CHOCOLATE PASTA

serves 6

1¾ cups	**all-purpose flour**	425 mL
¼ cup	**powdered chocolate**	50 mL
¼ cup	**sugar**	50 mL
5	**large eggs**	5
¼ cup	**melted dark chocolate**	125 mL

Sift together flour, powdered chocolate and sugar. Set aside. Beat the eggs and set aside. Melt chocolate in double boiler, when melted beat into eggs. Then add flour mixture, mix well and form dough into a ball. Cut dough into 6 pieces and put through pasta machine on medium setting; then put through pasta machine on spaghetti setting. Remember to dust both sides well. Cook chocolate pasta in water for 4-5 minutes or until al dente. Place cooked pasta on plate; top with berry sauce and a dollop of whipped cream. Garnish with a few fresh berries and chocolate curls.

berry sauce

¾ cup	**fresh strawberries**	175 mL
½ cup	**fresh raspberries**	125 mL
¼ cup	**sugar**	50 mL
½ tbsp.	**cornstarch**	7 mL
1 tbsp.	**cold water**	15 mL

Combine fruit and sugar in blender or food processor; blend until smooth. Put into saucepan; heat until warm, adding cornstarch and water mixture to thicken as needed.

wine selection

A late harvest Riesling from California.

CHOCOLATE TORTELLINI

with orange cream cheese filling

serves 6

1 recipe	Chocolate Pasta, page 112	1 recipe
1 cup	cream cheese	250 mL
¼ cup	sugar	50 mL
⅛ cup	Grand Marnier	25 mL
3	oranges, grated zest (rind) only	3
1	egg, beaten	1
1 cup	whipping cream	250 mL
	orange slices for garnish	
	white chocolate for garnish	

Roll out pasta and cut into 3" (7 cm) circles. Set aside. Beat cream cheese, sugar and Grand Marnier until smooth. Add orange zest. Take ½ tsp. (2 mL) of filling, place in center of tortellini and fold once in half. With a pastry brush, brush the open sides with beaten eggs. To seal, pinch sides together. Set aside. Drop tortellini, a few at a time, into boiling water. Boil until cooked, about 8-10 minutes. Drain. Whip cream until it forms soft peaks. Place 3 dollops of whipped cream on each dessert dish; then arrange 6 tortellini on plate. Serve with a slice of orange and grated white chocolate.

note

If you find that the orange filling is too soft, place in the refrigerator until it sets.

wine selection

Orange Muscat

A L L S P I C E   L A S A G N E

with fruit filling

serves 8

1 lb.	flour	500 g
3 tbsp.	allspice	45 mL
5	eggs	5

To make noodles, combine all ingredients and roll into a ball. Slice into 6 pieces. Roll as thin as possible in pasta machine. Cut into 12 strips, 8"-9" (20 cm-23 cm) long. Lay out to dry or cook 4-5 minutes, lay out on towel until needed.

note

When rolling in pasta machine, flour both sides well, otherwise it will stick.

fruit filling

¼ cup	orange juice	50 mL
3 cups	peeled, thinly sliced apples	750 mL
2 cups	peeled, thinly sliced pears	500 mL
1 cup	peeled, thinly sliced kiwi	250 mL
¾ cup	white sugar	175 mL
½ tsp.	vanilla	2 mL
½ tsp.	cinnamon	2 mL
	brown sugar	
	grated mild Cheddar cheese	
	whipped cream for garnish	
	mint leaves for garnish	

To make filling, combine orange juice, apples and pears in a pot; cover and steam for 10 minutes. Combine kiwi, sugar, vanilla and cinnamon with the apple mixture and set aside. Take a greased 8" x 8" x 2" (20 cm x 20 cm x 5 cm) pan and place 1 layer of noodles on the bottom; spread with a layer of fruit; a layer of noodles and so on until all the fruit is used. Top lasagne with brown sugar and grated mild Cheddar cheese. Bake in a 350°F (180°C) oven until cheese is melted, about 20-25 minutes. Serve and garnish with whipped cream and a fresh mint leaf.

E D I B L E F L O W E R S

Add flavor and flair to your food with beautiful, nutritious and flavorful edible flowers. For centuries, many cultures have used flowers as food and as edible garnishes. Experiment to satisfy your eye and your palate. Sprinkle mixed green salads with blossoms; float petals or flowers on individual servings of soup or in a glass of white wine; garnish appetizers, main courses or desserts with appropriate blossoms and leaves.

Anise-Hyssop — flowers and leaves

Bachelor's Button/Cornflower — flowers and leaves

Bellflower — flowers, leaves and root

Bergamot/Bee Balm/Oswego Tea — flowers and leaves

Borage — flowers and leaves

Calendula/Pot Marigold — petals and leaves

Camellia—petals

Carnation — petals

Chives/Garlic Chives —flowers and leaves

Chrysanthemum —petals

Dandelion — petals, leaves and root

Forsythia — flowers and leaves

Geranium — petals and leaves

Hollyhock — petals and leaves

Impatiens — flowers

Johnny-Jump-Up/Viola — flowers and leaves

Lavender — flowers

Lilac — flowers and leaves

Lilies — flowers; Day Lilies — flowers, stems buds and roots

Note: Lily-of-the Valley is poisonous

Marigold — petals

Nasturtium — buds, flowers and leaves

Orange Blossoms — petals

Pansy — flowers, stems and leaves

Peony — flowers and roots

Periwinkle/Myrtle — flowers and leaves

Petunia — flowers

Poppy **not** Opium—flowers, petals

Rose — flowers and hips

Sage/Clary Sage /Pineapple Sage — flowers and leaves

Snapdragon — flowers

Squash Blossoms — flowers

Tulip — flowers and bulbs

Zucchini Blossoms — flowers

Warning: Make sure that flowers have not been sprayed with pesticides.

Do Not Eat The Following Flowers—Aconite (Monkshood), Anemone, Azalea, Belladonna, Bleeding Heart, Buttercup, Clematis, Daffodil, Delphinium, Hyacinths, Jasmine (yellow), Lily-of-the-Valley, Lobelia, Morning Glory, Oleander, Poppy (red), Rhododendron, Rose (Christmas), Snowdrop.

I N D E X

Share *The Garden Gourmet's Vegetable Cookery*

Please send me_____copies of The Garden Gourmet's Vegetable Cookery at $9.95 per book plus
$2.00 (total order) for shipping and handling

    Number of books _____ x $9.95= $_____

    Postage and handling _____ = $_____ 2.00

    Subtotal _____ = $_____

    Please add G.S.T., if applicable, after Jan. 1, 1991 ____(x .07) = $_____

    Total enclosed _____ = $_____

        U.S. and international orders payable in U.S. funds. Price is subject to change.

NAME_____

STREET _____

CITY _____PROV./STATE _____

COUNTRY_____POSTAL CODE/ZIP _____

Please make cheque or money order payable to: **Garden Gourmet Enterprises**
                                         P.O. Box 78035
                                         Pharmasave
                                         Port Coquitlam, British Columbia
                                         Canada V3B 7H5

    For fund-raising or volume purchases, contact Garden Gourmet Enterprises for volume rates.
                        Please allow 3-4 weeks for delivery.

Share *The Garden Gourmet's Vegetable Cookery*

Please send me_____copies of The Garden Gourmet's Vegetable Cookery at $9.95 per book
plus $2.00 (total order) for shipping and handling

    Number of books _____ x $9.95= $_____

    Postage and handling _____ = $_____ 2.00

    Subtotal _____ = $_____

    Please add G.S.T., if applicable, after Jan. 1, 1991 ____(x .07) = $_____

    Total enclosed _____ = $_____

        U.S. and international orders payable in U.S. funds. Price is subject to change.

NAME _____

STREET _____

CITY _____PROV./STATE _____

COUNTRY_____POSTAL CODE/ZIP _____

Please make cheque or money order payable to: **Garden Gourmet Enterprises**
                                         P.O. Box 78035
                                       Pharmasave
                                         Port Coquitlam, British Columbia
                                       Canada V3B 7H5

    For fund-raising or volume purchases, contact Garden Gourmet Enterprises for volume rates.
                        Please allow 3-4 weeks for delivery.